CONTEMPORARY AUSTRALIAN POETRY

CONTEMPORARY AUSTRALIAN POETRY

AN ANTHOLOGY
Edited by John Leonard

Linda Magee
P.N.L
485 7531

Houghton Mifflin Australia

I am grateful to James Cook University of North Queensland
for financial assistance through a Special Research Grant
in the preparation of this anthology.

J. L.

Houghton Mifflin Australia Pty Ltd
PO Box 289, Ferntree Gully, Victoria 3156
112 Lewis Rd, Knoxfield, Victoria 3180, Australia

First published 1990
This collection copyright © John Leonard 1990
Individual poems copyright © as specified on the Acknowledgements pages

National Library of Australia
Cataloguing-in-Publication entry:

Contemporary Australian poetry.

ISBN 0 86770 113 7.

   1. Australian poetry — 20th century.
   I. Leonard, John, 1940 –   .

A821.308

Designed by Peter Shaw
Typeset in Caxton Light by Midland Typesetters, Victoria
Printed in Australia by Australian Print Group

Arts for
Australians
Australia Council

Publication assisted by the Australia Council,
the Federal Government's arts funding and advisory body

Contents

Introduction

In making this selection of poetry written by Australians during the past quarter-century or so, I am struck by the sheer scope of what has been written. Its note is one of confidence: this is an eloquent poetry, which discovers an abundance of voices and forms, and offers many perspectives on the contemporary world.

During this period, of course, Australia itself has become more open to variety. Its comparative isolation from 'overseas' influences has been broken by large-scale postwar immigration and the revolution in communications. These have enriched the dominant Anglo-Celtic culture, challenging a bulwark of that culture, its conformism. In retrospect, the taut metrical restraint so finely developed in the work of many Australian poets as they entered the 1960s — poets such as A.D. Hope, David Campbell, Judith Wright, James McAuley, Rosemary Dobson and Gwen Harwood — may be fairly seen as a natural expression of the inner control that pervaded much of the culture, while the poetry remained consciously at odds with the strain of anti-intellectualism in society at large. Its readers were, as often as not, associated with universities or with artistic 'bohemian' groupings.

By the early 1970s a change had occurred. Younger poets had established freer forms and dictions based on those that had long been in use in Europe and the Americas. The field of experience with which poetry might deal was opened out, and it began to reach a wider readership. Interestingly, most of the older poets adapted, and contributed to the freeing of forms. The classical forms, moreover, did not disappear entirely but became more flexible. Something of this complex transition may be traced in these pages.

What enabled this change technically was free verse — the line which is free of metrical constraints and improvises its rhythm and length. This mode had, of course, been used by poets in Australia before, but had tended to be labelled experimental. It was Bruce Dawe, perhaps more than any other poet, who got it accepted. By the early 1960s he had developed a controlled but supple line capable of bearing many tones, from the formal to the vernacular. This was a discursive style, one that struck a chord with readers because it so convincingly provided a language to describe the sharpness of ordinary experience. Dawe typically focused on the suburbs; Les Murray, who followed, wrote of the rural heartland. But the style is not a parochial one. What is distinctive about the free-verse discursive line is that it mingles vernacular language — rhythms and words that people use daily —with a wide vocabulary and reference. It is also highly adaptable. Robert Gray, for example, turns it to an almost painterly sensuous meditation.

It has become for many poets the 'middle style' of flexible poetic discourse which Hope had been seeking, and advocating, in rhymed pentameter. Pentameter, however, has tended, with a few exceptions, to be rather too finely balanced to carry the full vigour of vernacular language. For the past two decades, an ear for free verse has been developing, especially since the young have been reading and sometimes writing it at school; and it has proved to be an attractive medium because it is capable not only of including the various vernacular registers but also of catching their sophistication. For example, in the poems by Kate Llewellyn selected here, the phrases shape into one another with ironies, reticences, unexpected images — the mind is never still: yet the phrases are mainly those of every day. Moreover, the line-endings are used with delicacy — for weighing, for tension, for that easing space (whether a real pause or a mental check) which gives the next line room to begin with its own rhythm.

Free verse has been central not only to the discursive poetry of the period, but also to the more fragmented and allusive styles of modernism that have run parallel with it. Although modernist techniques of symbolism had a considerable influence on Australian poets from Brennan to Wright, until this quarter-century the more fragmentary modes had less impact, with the powerful exception of the work of Francis Webb. Webb, who wrote little after 1964, is represented here by three poems written at about that time, and by a very late poem. A number of the poets in this anthology are plainly influenced by him. European styles of modernism have also had an influence in recent years through the work of Dimitris Tsaloumas, Antigone Kefala and others. However, the most energetic break into modernism occurred as part of the youthful spirit of revolt which galvanized the late 1960s and early 1970s, when personal networks and small presses sustained a largely inner-urban movement in poetry where the medium was mainly the message: the breaking of old forms and taboos. Out of this has emerged, among other strands, a style that involves a heightened consciousness of language as a fabrication, and plays with the dislocation of cliché. At times this process runs near to a disengagement which closes off significance. However, in the hands of poets such as John Tranter, John Forbes, Gig Ryan and a number of others included here, it can be a poignant mode, opening a nerve to the surprise and danger that can lurk in the shifting spaces of language.

A notable feature of the period has been the impact of poetry by women. It may not always be important to tie poetry to gender; however, much of the most interesting recent poetry by women bears an acute awareness of female identity. The approaches are myriad, both discursive and modernist. Some poets rewrite myths in women's terms: Fay Zwicky and Diane Fahey, among several others represented here. Some adopt a spare style which gathers the unspoken around simple statement, and some write verse which is calculatedly full-blown: Dorothy Hewett, in these pages, does both. Such poetry has transformed the field in recent years, and the quality of the change may be felt in a reading of this selection.

A good number of the poets included here would be found in any anthology of the period, but I am not proposing a canon. There are poets not here whose work might easily have found a place, and some of the emphases could have been shaped differently. I have chosen to represent the period with an interesting variety of strong poems that work together to show off their differences. I should add that an overview of the recent past requires a clear sense of what is being done now: the weighting towards recent poems is therefore deliberate. Also, it seems to me, a number of poets whose work has been developing during this time are now producing some of their most interesting poems. The date at the foot of each poem is that of first inclusion in a book by the poet. There is usually a gap of up to five years (very occasionally more) between the writing and the collecting of a poem; nevertheless, these dates offer a guide. Brackets around a date indicate first periodical or anthology publication where the poem has not yet appeared in a collection. The titles of volumes of poetry named in the biographical sketches are usually the most recent and available. They are not meant to be comprehensive, but to suggest a first place to look if the reader wishes to follow up the work of a poet.

Most of these volumes, however, will not be in the local bookshop and will have to be ordered. Poetry may receive some of the literary prizes and grants, but in this country it is a well-regarded minority art, far from the central role it once shared with music and dance in pre-industrial societies. When Shelley wrote in 1821 that poetry may express 'the spirit of an age', he was heralding, as it turned out, an age where prose fiction would perform that function. Prose has proved to be a fluent instrument for imagining the maze of material and behavioural connections which hold together the vast and rickety structure of urban-centred, industrialized society. In Australia during the past quarter-century, writing and publishing have become a major industry. Prose narrative is at the centre, so much so that 'writer' now usually means 'writer of fiction' or of its cousin, biography. Literary studies in the universities, where the interest has long been evolving towards a broader field of cultural studies, increasingly fix on narrative as their natural object. And as the publishers, writers and reviewers all know, joined as they are on an ever more smartly organized round of Writers' Weeks, interviews and launchings, the reading public prefers prose narrative as something which structures the world.

Poetry has a more wayward and refractive relation to the present age in Australia than most prose fiction. In Alan Wearne's *The Nightmarkets*, for instance, the tangible utterance of verse turns a story of politics and personal lives into an energetic flux of conversational speech — jagged, ironic, dodgy, and with no need of resolution. Poetry can also open a sudden window, as in the work of Mark O'Connor, whose poetic brings the language to bear on ecology and biology, and throws into startling relief the extent to which most poetry avoids consideration of science, which is such a central discourse of our time. Again, Murray's 'The Buladelah-Taree Holiday Song Cycle' is open to the influence of Aboriginal culture in an unexpected way, when from an Aboriginal song cycle he adapts not the story but the structure: the rhythms of language and the rituals described are those of white Australia, but the circularities — the repetitions and namings — that turn out to be so well adapted to the subject are from the land's original inhabitants. In this country, of course, a vast poetry in hundreds of original languages has been lost. Moreover, the brutal marginalization of Aboriginal people over two centuries has, among much else, enabled too few of them to gain a command of the language of their conquerors. Only recently has it been recognized that Aboriginal accents and dialects of English have a power of their own. The four poets represented here all write with a sharp irony. For too long the voice has been simply unheard.

In our time, however much poetry may touch on the larger public issues, it remains obdurately centred on an assertion of individual experience. It is language returned to the body from its accustomed ethereal place in a fast-reading print culture — you can't read poetry with the flick of an eye. It is also language that revels in the arbitrariness of structure: poetry has always been consciously oblique. In fact, poetry is plainly important to many people, as anyone who teaches creative writing will testify. There is a primitive impulse to write it, although the writer may not have read much verse by others. One of the functions of the many small poetry groups and workshops that have sprung up is the provision of other work to look at, along with the idea that reading widely in poetry is an excellent way to internalize how language can behave in a poem. Workshop experience also confirms that nearly anyone with the inclination — and a modicum of guidance from an experienced hand — can write a poem that will shape an image; and that many people enjoy finding they can do so. Writing a poem, like writing a story, is a way of taking command.

It is significant, too, that regular poetry readings have maintained a presence since the 1960s, and in some centres have evolved a thriving dramatic dimension as 'performance poetry'. Poems which are read on the page in this anthology will in many cases have found an audience at such readings. Public utterance, moreover, is a great loosener of genres when poetry shares the platform with prose or song. During this period, for example, there has been an interest (unusual in a stressed language such as English, as distinct, say, from French) in writing short, oblique narrative in concentrated prose, a page or less when printed, the right length for a public reading. With one highly rhythmical exception in the writing of Ania Walwicz, however, the present selection stops just short of including such work. The decision is not entirely arbitrary. There are qualities which the use of verse (however free the verse) heightens from the habits of normal spoken language, but which prose to an extent subdues: strong repetition and the lateral association of ideas. The first is a means to the second. Repetition — of rhythm, sound, word, or the form of a phrase — activates the shaping of line upon line: the memory of one line as we read the next creates associative connections. This effect depends entirely on utterance, aloud or silent. The syntax of prose, on the other hand, modulates rhythm and associative patterns to the point where the mind is able to scan quickly. Good prose and good poetry both sound well when read aloud, but only prose can be read quickly on a page. In this anthology, my interest has been in bringing together writing which is poetry in the sense of language used obtrusively — which trips up the mind that tries to scan it quickly, and palpably demands utterance in order to signify its richness.

We are usually drawn first to a poem by a savouring of interesting words: whatever else the enjoyment of poetry may entail, it is equivalent to the young child's joy at the feeling of words in rhythm. It should not be a wrestle. If a poem is dense, we need to allow it time to sort out in the mind: a poem will often clarify of its own accord with the familiarity of a number of readings. A promising development in recent years has been the awareness on the part of teachers of the deadening nature of the 'comprehension' assignments which at one time blighted poetry for many readers in middle school. In the curriculum, poetry is increasingly allied with arts such as drama and debating, which foster the speaking of words outright, clearly and with a joy in the possession. There is no better way to comprehension. If students are sufficiently immersed in poetry in this way, the questions touching on comprehension — and on ideas of verbal and cultural implication — will arise naturally and force discussion. (There may be lessons here, also, for university teaching.) In daily life we constantly respond to a broad variety of verbal signals, many of them very subtle. In this anthology, some of the poetry is dense and some is immediately lucid. The way in is probably by way of the latter, but not necessarily. Both will delight.

John Leonard

A.D. Hope

b 1907, Cooma, south-eastern NSW. He taught English at Sydney Teachers' College from 1938, then at the University of Melbourne, and from 1951 at what became the ANU in Canberra, where he lives. He is also a noted critic. *A Late Picking* (1975), *Antechinus* (1981), *The Age of Reason* (1985).

Advice to Young Ladies

A.U.C. 334: about this date
For a sexual misdemeanour, which she denied,
The vestal virgin Postumia was tried.
Livy records it among affairs of state.

They let her off: it seems she was perfectly pure;
The charge arose because some thought her talk
Too witty for a young girl, her eyes, her walk
Too lively, her clothes too smart to be demure.

The Pontifex Maximus, summing up the case,
Warned her in future to abstain from jokes,
To wear less modish and more pious frocks.
She left the court reprieved, but in disgrace.

What then? With her the annalist is less
Concerned than what the men achieved that year:
Plots, quarrels, crimes, with oratory to spare!
I see Postumia with her dowdy dress,

Stiff mouth and listless step; I see her strive
To give dull answers. She had to knuckle down.
A vestal virgin who scandalized that town
Had fair trial, then they buried her alive.

Alive, bricked up in suffocating dark,
A ration of bread, a pitcher if she was dry,
Preserved the body they did not wish to die
Until her mind was quenched to the last spark.

How many the black maw has swallowed in its time!
Spirited girls who would not know their place;
Talented girls who found that the disgrace
Of being a woman made genius a crime;

How many others, who would not kiss the rod
Domestic bullying broke or public shame?
Pagan or Christian, it was much the same:
Husbands, St Paul declared, rank next to God.

Livy and Paul, it may be, never knew
That Rome was doomed; each spoke of her with pride.
Tacitus, writing after both had died,
Showed that whole fabric rotten through and through.

Historians spend their lives and lavish ink
Explaining how great commonwealths collapse
From great defects of policy — perhaps
The cause is sometimes simpler than they think.

It may not seem so grave an act to break
Postumia's spirit as Galileo's, to gag
Hypatia as crush Socrates, or drag
Joan as Giordano Bruno to the stake.

Can we be sure? Have more states perished, then,
For having shackled the enquiring mind,
Than those who, in their folly not less blind,
Trusted the servile womb to breed free men?

1969

Country Places

Hell, Hay and Booligal!

I glean them from signposts in these country places,
Weird names, some beautiful, more that make me laugh.
Driving to fat-lamb sales or to picnic races,
I pass their worshippers of the golden calf
And, in the dust of their Cadillacs, a latter-day Habbakuk
Rises in me to preach comic sermons of doom,
Crying: 'Woe unto Tocumwal, Teddywaddy, Tooleybuc!'
And: 'Wicked Wallumburrawang, your hour has come!'

But when the Four Horsemen ride their final muster
And my sinful country sinks in the fiery rain
One name shall survive the doom and the disaster
That fell on the foolish cities of the plain.
Like the three holy children or the salamander
One place shall sing and flourish in the fire:
It is Sweet Water Creek at Mullengandra
And there at the Last Day I shall retire.

Hypatia (c. 370–415) was an astronomer and mathematician recognized as head of the neo-Platonist school of philosophy in Alexandria. She was murdered by a Christian mob.

Hell, Hay and Booligal!: 'Hay and Hell and Booligal' is the title of a poem by Banjo Paterson.

When Numbugga shrieks to Burrumbuttock:
'The curse of Sodom comes upon us all!'
When Tumbarumba calls for spade and mattock
And they bury Hell and Hay in Booligal;
When the wrath of God is loosed upon Gilgandra
And Gulargambone burns red against the west,
To Sweet Water Creek at Mullengandra
I shall rise and flee away and be at rest.

When from Goonoo Goonoo, Underbool and Grong Grong
And Suggan Buggan there goes up the cry,
From Tittybong, Drik Drik and Drung Drung,
'Help, Lord, help us, or we die!'
I shall lie beside a willow-cool meander, or
Cut myself a fly-whisk in the shade,
And from Sweet Water Creek at Mullengandra
Fill my cup and whet my whistle unafraid.

When Boinka lies in ruins (more's the pity!),
And a heavenly trump proclaims the End of Grace,
With: 'Wombat is fallen, is fallen, that great city!'
Adding: 'Bunyip is in little better case';
When from Puckapunyal and from Yackandandah
The cry goes up: 'How long, O Lord, how long?'
I shall hear the she-oaks sough at Mullengandra
And the Sweet Waters ripple into song:

Oh, there's little to be hoped for Grabben Gullen
And Tumbulgum shrinks and shudders at its fate;
Folks at Wantabadgery and Cullen Bullen
Have Buckley's chance of reaching Heaven's gate;
It's all up with Cootamundra and Kiandra
And at Collarenebri they know they're through;
But at Sweet Water Creek at Mullengandra
You may pitch your camp and sleep the whole night through.

God shall punish Cargelligo, Come-by-Chance, Chinkapook;
They shall dance no more at Merrijig nor drink at Gentleman's Halt;
The sin of Moombooldool He shall in no wise overlook;
Wee Jasper and Little Jillaby, He shall not condone their fault;
But though I preach down Nap Nap and annihilate Narrandera,
One place shall yet be saved, this I declare:
Sweet Water Creek at Mullengandra
For its name and for my sake the Lord shall spare.

Coda

Alas! my beautiful, my prosperous, my careless country,
She destroys herself: the Lord will come too late!

They have cut down even their only tree at One Tree;
Dust has choked Honey Bugle and drifts over Creeper Gate;
The fires we lit ourselves on Mount Boothegandra
Have made more ruin than Heaven's consuming flame;
Even Sweet Water Creek at Mullengandra,
If I went there now, would it live up to its name?

1975

In Memoriam: Gertrud Kolmar, 1943

Immer sind wir Blaubarts Frauen.

Whistling past this cemetery in the dark
Where most of your generation lie interred,
I think of Francis Bacon's *jeu d'esprit*:
'Kings are God's playfellows.' The great bone-park
Chuckles and rattles as if the dead had heard.
'Kings play at dangerous games.' They all agree,

We are proof that kings play a *very* dangerous game.
In a match against God, someone is bound to get hurt!
What was He doing, the morning they took you away,
For having a loving heart and a Jewish name,
While a king with a swastika badge on a brown shirt
Captained the opposite team and called the play?

Where was He, too, that night you mused in the dark,
Dog-tired, half-starved, the Terror just closing round,
Taking incredible comfort from St. Just's joke:
'Men perish that God may live'? Did His Covenant Ark
Go before you to Auschwitz, his ram's-horn sound
Till the gas-chambers of Jericho breached and broke?

When they knocked you down and a jackboot kicked in your teeth,
Did you sing with Job: 'Though He slay me, yet will I trust'?
Or did you remember St. Just and the poem you made,
That gay, that terrible poem confronting death:
'We have always been Bluebeard's wives; we always must!'?
That was your answer to God and games he played.

Gertrud Kolmar, a German-Jewish poet, was killed by the Nazis, probably at Auschwitz. Shortly before, while still in her home but knowing what was coming, she wrote how she had lain in the dark and 'applied . . . to everything, to all occurrences, the measure of eternity . . . "Peoples die that God may live": this remark of St. Just came to mind.' Hope's epigraph here comes from the opening line of one of her poems: 'Ever are we Wives of Bluebeard'.

We were all contracted, but we discovered instead
Once married that God was Bluebeard after all.
He had left on a journey, trusting us with a Key
To his universe. Alone in His double bed,
We wondered about that cupboard in the hall,
A forbidden closet, like the forbidden tree.

He had kissed us with lips that curved like scimitars,
Blood-red they smiled out of that blue-black beard.
The huge male bush hung over us like a threat;
Yet we knew we loved and were loved. The universe
Rang with His power and His love. When He disappeared
The Key was our comfort, His kiss a sign that He would not forget.

For love was our shield; love was our talisman;
Love was our guide the day we decided to use the Key.
So we crept to His closet door and opened it just a crack;
And there we saw clearly the whole condition of man.
Now we know the meaning of Bluebeard's love, and we
Quake in His castle of dread — pray that he will not come back.

But to whom do we pray? There is nobody else to hear.
Bluebeard is bound to return; He has heard our prayer.
He will come loving and smiling; ask for that blood-spotted key
While we cower in the bed of despair, that last, lost outpost of fear.
But you, you alone will stand up; you will teach us to dare;
You will teach us that calm at the worst, when the spirit goes free.

Whistling past your cemetery in the black
Storm of our century of hate and dread,
I, who have lived in shelter all of my days,
Bring you, before the Lord of the Keys gets back,
Word from all those still doomed to those who are already dead,
Those able to recognize all and yet still able to praise.

Stand back now, Azrael: I have a few moments yet.
You can have this carcass when I have had my say.
Yet what can I say for her, who said nothing at all
But dressed for her death like a bride: who paid the debt
Of the ancient doom of her race without dismay;
Who went to that doom as though to a festival?

All we can do, perhaps, is not to forget.

(Bluebeard is back! I have heard his step in the hall.)

1975

Inscription for a War

Stranger, go tell the Spartans
we died here obedient to their commands.
Inscription at Thermopylae

Linger not, stranger; shed no tear;
Go back to those who sent us here.

We are the young they drafted out
To wars their folly brought about.

Go tell those old men, safe in bed,
We took their orders and are dead.

1981

Elizabeth Riddell

b 1910, Napier, NZ; arrived in Australia at eighteen. She has worked since then as a journalist, in Sydney and abroad. *Selected Poems* (1991).

Security

for Elaine Haxton

Luckily, they do not make new flowers,
only variations of the same.

Rock stays the same and waves and sand
and paint on your canvas or your board,
so there is security.

While you finish this triptych
(the view from Mountadam, trees and sky)
and brush in your name
Claudio Arrau plays the notes as ever
pressing them from black to white,
distilling them in drops from his finger tips
with such deliberation
that fast is slow.

Luckily, all cats stretch the same way,
one, two, three, four, the legs and back
uncoiled, then arced and
with averted yellow gaze, privately.

Things grow in their way, angular or loose
whoever plants them. The colour of flame seldom changes
or the beginning of day
which is pale and tentative, with a meek light
no matter what comes after.
So there is security. Look for no more.

1987

Possibilities in an Airplane

Look after yourself, you said. For you, for me?
For voyages, for a mountain, for the moon?
Look after what — this flesh lying quiet in the dark,
an effigy that disbelieves the imminent light,
knowing dogs chase the shadows with delinquent bark
lifting their sullen muzzles to the sky?
Look after blood that hesitates between the tissues
then stumbles, seeps and stops?

Better wish me the ending of a long dry season,
that this blood reconstitute to bloody rain,
the riverbed reshape to dreams of flood,
wish banks to brim with weed and fish and fern
and that the One who squats above us in a tower of fire and ice
should lean down and burn
the crust from the closed wound.

I mark, from two miles up in cloud, where you live now
(sending me your treacherous wishes) with rocks and trees
where crows go lurching by
a horse that rolls and flourishes his hooves
at lounging cattle by the old scummed wells.

I wish this great machine would fall and flutter
as a flower or a feather on your roof
to end your subversive wishing. I will not deny
myself the sight of the bird of paradise nor forgo
my last glimpse of the leaping unicorn.

1987

Barbara Giles

b 1912, Manchester, UK; arrived in Australia 1923. She has been a schoolteacher and is also a writer for children. She lives in Melbourne. *Earth and Solitude* (1984), *The Hag in the Mirror* (1989).

Learning All the Words in the World

for Fabian

Walking accomplished, so much energy
goes into words. Each object named
with glee, each name a part of object,
each object recollectable by name
for her admiring listeners.

She sits on the edge of conversation,
practising. 'Shattered,' she says and 'Tipsy,'
'Wild goose chase,' 'Naive.' The talkers
glance at her and stop their talk of rape,
rummaging in memory for paradigms
of infant apperception. One recalls
fear, of a gaggle of geese, the other, blame,
defiance, ashes in the mouth.

They cease to scold, sweetening their words, but soon
they're back to what's more natural to them,
rapping the world from pot to politics.
The child turns pages carefully, intoning,
'Apple: fish: jaguar: peacock: unicorn.'
Studious, prim, 'Nuclear war,' she says.

1984

Fireworks and Champagne

I pass among you disguised, you'll scarcely see me
in this slack envelope, unremarkable,

heavy with the dull purviews of age,
warmth, the next meal, the next step.

Ah, if you knew, I am in my second childhood,
each flower incandescent, the sky bluer and bluer.

Spring is a star-burst, the trees whizz up like rockets,
the children are jumping-jacks, girls are fountains.

Such color and sound, I shall shatter with joy,
leach into rivers, blow on the wind.

You can sweep me up, walk through me,
I am winning, I am becoming invisible.

1984

Almost out of Breath

I hear your far voice with terrible
clarity. You ask am I ready
to travel outside these pitiful limits,
taking the unreckoned journey, making

the new sweet acquaintance
of one who, compassionate,
averts his bright face, having
no need to name himself.

I'll come at the very first call, only please,
ask him to hold out his hand.

This is a very strange country.

1989

John Blight

b 1913, Adelaide. He has spent most of his life in areas of south-eastern Queensland, working variously as an orchardist, an accountant and a part-owner of sawmills. He lives in Brisbane. *Selected Poems* (1976), *Pageantry for a Lost Empire* (1977)

The Spit

It is undersea half-tide, it is land
at low; and people walk out on it
gathering bailer shells, and helmet shells, and
all kinds of jetsam washed up on the spit.
Some day, the seers say, they'll make something out of it.
They'll dredge the channel, pump the sand,
and build it up, raise the spit
above the tide till it's all dry land;
then fill in the shoals behind the spit.
All's been blue-printed, thoroughly planned:
the cubic yards of shell and grit.
To those few fellows who beachcombed it,
and found life's solace on the spit,
it will be banned, it will be banned.

1968

Bee's Sting

That was a very bad year, when
I remember the wincing visit of a
grocer — grocers visiting for orders
and thereafter payment and,
thereafter, again . . .

                        but the ranunculi
were flowering almost without attention and,
pink-eyed, I realised the terror of
debt in a flowering society, where
the bees had no care, unless I foolishly
trapped one and it stung — and
when it stung, I learnt, its sting was
left in me and . . . it flew away and
died.

            I have, ever since, been considerate
of bees . . . and, our grocer was a
kind man. I didn't know why
he wasn't paid, many times; and, yet,
I ate the jam and dripping he
brought to us. Oh, I knew debt, young,
when nobody perceived it; and the
bee's sting left in me made me sorry
and soft-hearted for a loser.

                        I try now
not to eat, if I owe a beggar crumbs.

                                                1975

David Campbell

1915-79; b Ellerslie Station, near Adelong, south-eastern NSW (now ACT). He farmed in the district, after wartime service as a pilot. *Collected Poems* (1989).

The Australian Dream

The doorbell buzzed. It was past three o'clock.
The steeple-of-Saint-Andrew's weathercock
Cried silently to darkness, and my head
Was bronze with claret as I rolled from bed
To ricochet from furniture. Light! Light
Blinded the stairs, the hatstand sprang upright,
I fumbled with the lock, and on the porch
Stood the Royal Family with a wavering torch.

'We hope,' the Queen said, 'we do not intrude.
The pubs were full, most of our subjects rude.
We came before our time. It seems the Queen's
Command brings only, "Tell the dead marines!"
We've come to you.' I must admit I'd half
Expected just this visit. With a laugh
That put them at their ease, I bowed my head.
'Your Majesty is most welcome here,' I said.
'My home is yours. There is a little bed
Downstairs, a boiler-room, might suit the Duke.'
He thanked me gravely for it and he took
Himself off with a wave. 'Then the Queen Mother?
She'd best bed down with you. There is no other
But my wide bed. I'll curl up in a chair.'
The Queen looked thoughtful. She brushed out her hair
And folded up *The Garter* on a pouf.
'Distress was the first commoner, and as proof
That queens bow to the times,' she said, 'we three
Shall share the double bed. Please follow me.'

I waited for the ladies to undress —
A sense of fitness, even in distress,
Is always with me. They had tucked away
Their state robes in the lowboy; gold crowns lay
Upon the bedside tables; ropes of pearls
Lassoed the plastic lampshade; their soft curls
Were spread out on the pillows and they smiled.
'Hop in,' said the Queen Mother. In I piled
Between them to lie like a stick of wood.
I couldn't find a thing to say. My blood
Beat, but like rollers at the ebb of tide.
'I hope your Majesties sleep well,' I lied.
A hand touched mine and the Queen said, 'I am
Most grateful to you, Jock. Please call me Ma'am.'

1968

Snake

The tiger snake moves
Like slow lightning. Like
A yard of creek water
It flows over rocks
Carving the grass.

Where have you gone,
Long fellow, cold brother,

Like a lopped limb or
Truth that we shy from
Leaving a cast skin?

Snakes are like a line
Of poetry: a chill
Wind in the noon,
A slalom in the spine
Setting ears back, hair on end.

'Some people will not live
With a snake in the house.'
Mice make off. Look
Under your chair; worse
Take down a book:

A line like an icicle!

1975

Crab

The crab sidled out
From its hiding place
Beneath my shoulder-blade

Fending with one enlarged claw
It scuttled sideways
And settled in an outcropping elbow

It left tiptoe tracks
In the hard sands of the ulna
Pain broke on the white beach

The crab has reached my hand
In the dreck at the high-tide line
Look what I have found.

1979

August

Snowgums glitter like ice
And icicles
Litter like glass the snow.
Led by buried water
A fox digs
With snarled-back lips
And cracks the ice-green crayfish.

And like a fern
A lyrebird trembles in the wind
On the black and white range.
His winter passion
Shrill with the mating calls
Of silent birds
Rings like water under snow.

1979

Clarinets

Early risers
Clarinets are out
Defining a territory

They muse in blue trees
The meditations
Of benign madmen

Glory the clarinets
Cry from a bough
And shake the spit out

Glory they cry
To the farmer in the morning
Milking his manna

Glory — a clarinet
Blows by my ear
Knocking my hat off.

1979

Judith Wright

b 1915, Thalgarrah Station, near Armidale, north-eastern NSW. She is a prominent environ-
mentalist and advocate of Aboriginal rights, and lives at Mongarlowe, south-eastern NSW.
A Human Pattern: Selected Poems (1990).

A Document

'Sign there.' I signed, but still uneasily.
I sold the coachwood forest in my name.
Both had been given me; but all the same
remember that I signed uneasily.

Ceratopetalum, Scented Satinwood:
a tree attaining seventy feet in height.

Those pale-red calyces like sunset light
burned in my mind. A flesh-pink pliant wood

used in coachbuilding. Difficult of access
(those slopes were steep). But it was World War Two.
Their wood went into bomber-planes. They grew
hundreds of years to meet those hurried axes.

Under our socio-legal dispensation
both name and woodland had been given me.
I was much younger then than any tree
matured for timber. But to help the nation

I signed the document. The stand was pure
(eight hundred trees perhaps). Uneasily
(the bark smells sweetly when you wound the tree)
I set upon this land my signature.

1966

Eve to Her Daughters

It was not I who began it.
Turned out into draughty caves,
hungry so often, having to work for our bread,
hearing the children whining,
I was nevertheless not unhappy.
Where Adam went I was fairly contented to go.
I adapted myself to the punishment: it was my life.

But Adam, you know . . . !
He kept on brooding over the insult,
over the trick They had played on us, over the scolding.
He had discovered a flaw in himself
and he had to make up for it.

Outside Eden the earth was imperfect,
the seasons changed, the game was fleet-footed,
he had to work for our living, and he didn't like it.
He even complained of my cooking
(it was hard to compete with Heaven).

So he set to work.
The earth must be made a new Eden
with central heating, domesticated animals,
mechanical harvesters, combustion engines,
escalators, refrigerators,

and modern means of communication
and multiplied opportunities for safe investment
and higher education for Abel and Cain
and the rest of the family.
You can see how his pride had been hurt.

In the process he had to unravel everything,
because he believed that mechanism
was the whole secret — he was always mechanical-minded.
He got to the very inside of the whole machine
exclaiming as he went, So this is how it works!
And now that I know how it works, why, I must have invented it.
As for God and the Other, they cannot be demonstrated,
and what cannot be demonstrated.
doesn't exist.
You see, he had always been jealous.

Yes, he got to the centre
where nothing at all can be demonstrated.
And clearly he doesn't exist; but he refuses
to accept the conclusion.
You see, he was always an egotist.

It was warmer than this in the cave;
there was none of this fall-out.
I would suggest, for the sake of the children,
that it's time you took over.

But you are my daughters, you inherit my own faults of character;
you are submissive, following Adam
even beyond existence.
Faults of character have their own logic
and it always works out.
I observed this with Abel and Cain.

Perhaps the whole elaborate fable
right from the beginning
is meant to demonstrate this; perhaps it's the whole secret.
Perhaps nothing exists but our faults?
At least they can be demonstrated.

But it's useless to make
such a suggestion to Adam.
He has turned himself into God,
who is faultless, and doesn't exist.

1966

Portrait

It was a heartfelt game, when it began —
polish and cook and sew and mend, contrive,
move between sink and stove, keep flower-beds weeded —
all her love needed was that it was needed,
and merely living kept the blood alive.

Now an old habit leads from sink to stove,
mends and keeps clean the house that looks like home,
and waits in hunger dressed to look like love
for the calm return of those who, when they come,
remind her: this was a game, when it began.

1966

Tableau

Bent over, staggering in panic or despair
from post to parking-meter in the hurried street,
he seemed to gesture at me,
as though we had met again; had met somewhere
forgotten, and now for the last time had to meet.

And I debated with myself; ought I to go
over the road — since no one stopped to ask
or even stand and look —
abandon my own life awhile and show
I was too proud to shirk that ant-like task?

And finally went. His almost vanished voice
accepted me; he gave himself to my hold,
(*pain, cancer — keep me still*).
We leaned on a drinking-fountain, fused in the vice
of a double pain; his sweat dropped on me cold.

Holding him up as he asked till the ambulance came,
among the sudden curious crowd, I knew
his plunging animal heart,
against my flesh the shapes of his too-young bone,
the heaving pattern of ribs. As still I do.

Warding the questioners, bearing his rack of weight,
I drank our strange ten minutes of embrace,
and watched him whiten there,
the drenched poverty of his slender face.
We could have been desperate lovers met too late.

1973

from *The Shadow of Fire: Ghazals*

Oppositions

Today I was caught alone in a summer storm
counting heartbeats from flash to crash of thunder.

From a small plane once I looked down a cliff of cloud.
Like God to Moses, it exploded into instructions.

Home, a yellow frog on the shower-pipe
startled my hand and watched me as I watch lightning.

Frog, my towel is wet, my hair dripping,
but you don't for such reasons take me to be a refuge.

Small damp peaceful sage with a loony grin,
('one minute of sitting, one inch of Buddha')

a long time back we clambered up the shore
and learned to play with fire. Now there's no stopping us.

Back to the drainpipe, frog, don't follow me.
I'm off to dry my hair by the radiator.

I can't believe that wine's warm solaces
don't help the searcher: the poet on the wineshop floor

was given his revelations. The hermit of Cold Mountain
laughs as loudly perhaps — I choose fire, not snow.

Skins

This pair of skin gloves is sixty-six years old,
mended in places, worn thin across the knuckles.

Snakes get rid of their coverings all at once.
Even those empty cuticles trouble the passer-by.

Counting in seven-year rhythms I've lost nine skins
though their gradual flaking isn't so spectacular.

Holding a book or a pen I can't help seeing
how age crazes surfaces. Well, and interiors?

You ask me to read those poems I wrote in my thirties?
They dropped off several incarnations back.

1985

'*one minute of sitting . . .*': from Manzan (1635-1714). *The Hermit of Cold Mountain*: Han-shan (7th or 8th century), Chinese poet.

Smalltown Dance

Two women find the square-root of a sheet.
That is an ancient dance:
arms wide: together: again: two forward steps: hands meet
your partner's once and twice.
That white expanse
reduces to a neat
compression fitting in the smallest space
a sheet can pack in on a cupboard shelf.

High scented walls there were of flapping white
when I was small, myself.
I walked between them, playing Out of Sight.
Simpler than arms, they wrapped and comforted —
clean corridors of hiding, roofed with blue —
saying, Your sins too are made Monday-new;
and see, ahead
that glimpse of unobstructed waiting green.
Run, run before you're seen.

But women know the scale of possibility,
the limit of opportunity,
the fence,
how little chance
there is of getting out. The sheets that tug
sometimes struggle from the peg,
don't travel far. Might symbolise
something. Knowing where danger lies
you have to keep things orderly.
The household budget will not stretch to more.

And they can demonstrate it in a dance.
First pull those wallowing white dreamers down,
spread arms: then close them. Fold
those beckoning roads to some impossible world,
put them away and close the cupboard door.

1985

Jack Davis

b 1917, Perth, of Aboriginal, part-Sikh, part-Irish descent. His many occupations have included stockman, lay preacher and actor. Also a playwright, and a prominent spokesman for Aboriginal rights, he lives in Fremantle, WA. *The First-born* (1970), *John Pat* (1988).

Camped in the Bush

Wind in the hair
Of a sleeping child
And the tree-tops wavering,
The starlight mild.

The moon's first peep
On the sand-plain rise,
And the fox in the shadows
With flashing eyes.

Over the campfire
The bat cries shrill
And a 'semi' snarls
On the Ten Mile Hill.

And the lonely whistle
Of the train at night,
Where my kingdom melted
In the city's light.

1970

John Pat

John Pat was a 16-year-old Aboriginal boy who died of head injuries alleged to have been caused in a disturbance between police and Aborigines in Roebourne, WA, in 1983. Four police were charged with manslaughter over the incident. They were acquitted.

Write of life
the pious said
forget the past
the past is dead.
But all I see
in front of me
is a concrete floor
a cell door
and John Pat.

Agh! tear out the page
forget his age
thin skull they cried
that's why he died!
But I can't forget
the silhouette
of a concrete floor
a cell door
and John Pat.

The end product
of Guddia law
is a viaduct
for fang and claw,
and a place to dwell
like Roebourne's hell
of a concrete floor
a cell door
and John Pat.

He's there — where?
there in their minds now
deep within,
there to prance
a sidelong glance
a silly grin
to remind them all
of a Guddia wall
a concrete floor
a cell door
and John Pat.

1988

James McAuley

1917–76; b Sydney. He was a government adviser on New Guinea affairs, and from 1961 taught English at the University of Tasmania. He was also a noted editor and critic. *James McAuley: Poetry, Essays and Personal Commentary* (1988).

Pietà

A year ago you came
Early into the light.
You lived a day and night,
Then died; no-one to blame.

Guddia: Kimberley term for white man.

Once only, with one hand,
Your mother in farewell
Touched you. I cannot tell,
I cannot understand

A thing so dark and deep,
So physical a loss:
One touch, and that was all

She had of you to keep.
Clean wounds, but terrible,
Are those made with the Cross.

1969

Because

My father and my mother never quarrelled.
They were united in a kind of love
As daily as the *Sydney Morning Herald*,
Rather than like the eagle or the dove.

I never saw them casually touch,
Or show a moment's joy in one another.
Why should this matter to me now so much?
I think it bore more hardly on my mother,

Who had more generous feeling to express.
My father had dammed up his Irish blood
Against all drinking praying fecklessness,
And stiffened into stone and creaking wood.

His lips would make a switching sound, as though
Spontaneous impulse must be kept at bay.
That it was mainly weakness I see now,
But then my feelings curled back in dismay.

Small things can pit the memory like a cyst:
Having seen other fathers greet their sons,
I put my childish face up to be kissed
After an absence. The rebuff still stuns

My blood. The poor man's curt embarrassment
At such a delicate proffer of affection
Cut like a saw. But home the lesson went:
My tenderness thenceforth escaped detection.

My mother sang *Because,* and *Annie Laurie,*
White Wings, and other songs; her voice was sweet.
I never gave enough, and I am sorry;
But we were all closed in the same defeat.

People do what they can; they were good people,
They cared for us and loved us. Once they stood
Tall in my childhood as the school, the steeple.
How can I judge without ingratitude?

Judgment is simply trying to reject
A part of what we are because it hurts.
The living cannot call the dead collect:
They won't accept the charge, and it reverts.

It's my own judgment day that I draw near,
Descending in the past, without a clue,
Down to that central deadness: the despair
Older than any hope I ever knew.

                                                                  1969

Childhood Morning — Homebush

The half-moon is a muted lamp
Motionless behind a veil.
As the eastern sky grows pale,
I hear the slow-train's puffing stamp

Gathering speed. A bulbul sings,
Raiding persimmon and fig.
The rooster in full glossy rig
Crows triumph at the state of things.

I make no comment; I don't know;
I don't know what there is to know.
I hear that every answer's No,
But can't believe it can be so.

                                                                  1971

Nocturne

A gull flies low across the darkening bay.
Along the shore the casuarinas sigh.
Resentful plovers give their ratcheting cry
From the mown field scattered with bales of hay.

The world sinks out of sight. The moon congealed
In cloud seems motionless. The air is still.
A cry goes out from the exhausted will.
Nightmares and angels roam the empty field.

                                                                  1976

Anne Elder

1918–76; b Auckland, NZ; arrived in Australia aged three. As Anne MacIntosh, she was a soloist with the Borovansky Ballet. She farmed at Kilmore, central Victoria. *For the Record* (1972), *Crazy Woman* (1976).

The Love Fight

Spring is a waft, an outcry
of raw green, and the sun's hand
on the small of the back saying
Remember this ache? . . . it is birth.

Then the shock of starlings fighting
with savagery in the sweet morning.
An outrage that these who were newly
feathered in fire for the season
and oiled with the tints of dew
should be victim and conqueror spun
staggering like spent shuttlecocks
pivoted queerly on round heads . . .
until I saw that they were joined.

He changed grip, gagging her beak to her bosom,
and crippling the legs with a spare claw
shuffled her, swept her on the hard stones
glued to his breast as a freak twin,
to fall locked in the round grating
of a drain, and in that unlovely bed
he got her, got her properly with prolonged
repetitive impact counted
by the rhythmic spasm of a wing,
as she, undone, succumbed
totally unbirdlike, soft as a woman.
They were silent, there was no cry.

The whole act was hushed in feather,
shone with the stringent fitness of a wing
to denote the urge of life, and held
me ravished, curious as a child
under the old bland wink of spring that quickens
the viscid sappy vitriol of love.

1972

The Two Sides

for Philip Martin

Round about six of a summer's evening they come home
and turn into neighbours, the young Malays with dark eyes
who have sloped through warm streets from the university
— small people not in height but in size of hip and shoe.
　　　　　They make themselves known.
Suddenly a vile companionable odour of garlic fried
in a cauldron arises four feet from our noses. The fence
is high in this suburb of genteel tenements
but nothing can snub or silence them.
　　　　　A flock of currawongs
warbles amicably in their voices. One plays a thin flute.
One has a wife who moves easily seen from a top window.
They air themselves for an hour and retire.
　　　　　In the sudden calm
the spinsters on the other side proffer their noiselessness
— nice women with a trim garden that gives nothing away.

1972

Rosemary Dobson

b 1920, Sydney. She worked in Sydney as a book editor, and, after a period in London, moved to Canberra in 1972. *Selected Poems* (1991).

Autobiography

Time holds the glass the wrong way round:
I see a matchstick child, thin,
Dwindling through far-off summer days
Exhausted in a cotton dress,
Sustained by longing, burning still
With passion underneath the skin
For love, for words, for excellence.

She crouches over poetry,
Starts like a bird and trembling waits
The lightning-flash of love, exchange
Of name for name and known for known.
She learns that word and love are one
Though each assume a different form,
And she the seeker and the sought.

The good, indifferent and bad
She takes with equal joy, content
That all are shaped like poetry
And all can teach her excellence.
Now, chin on hand, I watch her make
Her wilful way to where I am.
How thin she is! How thin and grave!

1973

The Spring of Naupaktos

I think I'll take a journey to that spring
beside the sanctuary of Asklepios.
The water falling from the bare rock-face

might cleanse my eyes, as thinking of it strains
some darkness from my mind — a cloudiness —
and all is clear again. Pausanias

finding the sanctuary despoiled took
as in a phial this story from the spring.
It is the story of Phalysios

who built the sanctuary in thankfulness.
(The rhymes that sound in music through this tale
are random grace-notes scattered so to bless

with sound a poem celebrating sight —
the precious gift denied Phalysios.)
Sightless he cried upon Asklepios.

Asklepios replied oracularly
sending Anyte, poet, as messenger.
(I like the entrance here of Poetry.)

Pausanias says the god had given her
a tablet sealed and written, in a dream.
She woke and found the tablet in her hands.

Without demur she sailed to Naupaktos
and gave the tablet to Phalysios
bidding him read the contents and address.

(Anyte — what a girl she was! I wish
she was my sister of my time and place,
I think we would have tried each other's pace.)

Pausanias: author of *Guide to Greece*, 2nd century AD.

Phalysios did exactly as she said:
removed the seal and, looking at the wax,
received his sight — and this is what he read:

The bearer must be given, wrote the god,
two thousand coins in gold. Phalysios
bestowed the tribute on the charming girl.

She had her recompense; Phalysios
his sight; the god his sanctuary;
Pausanias his story; and I this.

1973

Canberra Morning

Morning: such long shadows
Like low-bellied cats
Creep under parked cars
And out again, stealthily
Flattening the grasses.

At the bus-stop
A flock of starlings:
School-children, chatterers,
Swinging haversacks,
Pulling ribbons.

The driver's got a book by
Sartre in his pocket,
He wears dark glasses,
Listens moodily
To the Top Forty.

Life gets better
As I grow older
Not giving a damn
And looking slantwise
At everyone's morning.

1973

The Nightmare

for C.S.

I sit beside the bed where she lies dreaming
Of pyrrhic victories and sharp words said,
She will annihilate the hospital

C.S.: Australian novelist Christina Stead.

She will destroy the medical profession
And, kicking her feet free, walk into the world.
She moves her fist to her mouth as a child does.

Suppose her smouldering thoughts break out in flame
Not to consume bed, nightdress, flesh and hair
But the mind, the working and the making mind

That built those towers which the world applauds,
And leave upon the bed this breathing body
Scarred with the rage and trouble of her time?

I have dreamt her nightmare for her. She wakes up
And turns to smile with quick complicity,
'I wasn't asleep. I watched you sitting there.'

1984

Gwen Harwood

b 1920, Brisbane; moved to Hobart 1945 and lives there, at Oyster Cove. She is also a librettist and musician. *Selected Poems* (3rd edn, 1990).

Barn Owl

[from *Father and Child*]

Daybreak: the household slept.
I rose, blessed by the sun.
A horny fiend, I crept
out with my father's gun.
Let him dream of a child
obedient, angel-mild —

old No-Sayer, robbed of power
by sleep. I knew my prize
who swooped home at this hour
with daylight-riddled eyes
to his place on a high beam
in our old stables, to dream

light's useless time away.
I stood, holding my breath,
in urine-scented hay,
master of life and death,
a wisp-haired judge whose law
would punish beak and claw.

My first shot struck. He swayed,
ruined, beating his only
wing, as I watched, afraid
by the fallen gun, a lonely
child who believed death clean
and final, not this obscene

bundle of stuff that dropped,
and dribbled through loose straw
tangling in bowels, and hopped
blindly closer. I saw
those eyes that did not see
mirror my cruelty

while the wrecked thing that could
not bear the light nor hide
hobbled in its own blood.
My father reached my side,
gave me the fallen gun.
'End what you have begun.'

I fired. The blank eyes shone
once into mine, and slept.
I leaned my head upon
my father's arm, and wept,
owl-blind in early sun
for what I had begun.

1975

Night Thoughts: Baby & Demon

Baby I'm sick. I need
nursing. Give me your breast.
My orifices bleed.
I cannot sleep. My chest
shakes like a window. Light
guts me. My head's not right.

Demon, we're old, old chap.
Born under the same sign
after some classic rape.
Gemini. Yours is mine.
Sickness and health. We'll share
the end of this affair.

Baby, I'm sick to death.
But I can't die. You do
the songs, you've got the breath.

Give them the old soft shoe.
Put on a lovely show.
Put on your wig, and go.

The service station flags, denticulate
plastic, snap in the wind. Hunched seabirds wait

for light to quench the unmeaning lights of town.
This day will bring the fabulous summer down.

Weather no memory can match will fade
to memory, leaf-drift in the pines' thick shade.

All night salt water stroked and shaped the sand.
All night I heard it. Your bravura hand

chimed me to shores beyond time's rocking swell.
The last cars leave the shabby beach motel.

Lovers and drunks unroofed in sobering air
disperse, ghost-coloured in the streetlight-glare.

    Rock-a-bye Baby
      in the motel
    Baby will kiss
      and Demon will tell.

One candle lights us. Night's cool airs begin
to lick the luminous edges of our skin.

    When the bough bends
      the apple will fall
    Baby knows nothing
      Demon knows all.

Draw up the voluptuously crumpled sheet.
In rose-dark silence gentle tongues repeat
the body's triumph through its grand eclipse.
I feel your pulsebeat through my fingertips.

    Baby's a rocker
      lost on the shore.
    Demon's a mocker.
      Baby's a whore.

World of the happy, innocent and whole:
the body's the best picture of the soul
couched like an animal in savage grace.
Ghost after ghost obscures your sleeping face.

My baby's like a bird of day
    that flutters from my side,
my baby's like an empty beach
    that's ravished by the tide.

So fair are you, my bonny lass,
    so sick and strange am I,
that I must lie with all your loves
    and suck your sweetness dry.

And drink your juices dry, my dear,
    and grind your bones to sand,
then I will walk the empty shore
    and sift you through my hand.

And sift you through my hand, my dear,
    and find you grain by grain,
and build your body bone by bone
    and flesh those bones again,

with flesh from all your loves, my love,
    while tides and seasons stream,
until you wake by candle-light
    from your midsummer dream,

and like some gentle creature meet
    the huntsman's murderous eye,
and know you never shall escape
    however fast you fly.

Unhoused I'll shout my drunken songs
    and through the streets I'll go
compelling all I meet to toast
    the bride they do not know.

Till all your tears are dry, my love,
    and your ghosts fade in the sun.
Be sure I'll have your heart, my love,
    when all your loving's done.

1975

Mother Who Gave Me Life

Mother who gave me life
I think of women bearing
women. Forgive me the wisdom
I would not learn from you.

It is not for my children I walk
on earth in the light of the living.
It is for you, for the wild
daughters becoming women,

anguish of seasons burning
backward in time to those other
bodies, your mother, and hers
and beyond, speech growing stranger

on thresholds of ice, rock, fire,
bones changing, heads inclining
to monkey bosom, lemur breast,
guileless milk of the word.

I prayed you would live to see
Halley's Comet a second time.
The Sister said, When she died
she was folding a little towel.

You left the world so, having lived
nearly thirty thousand days:
a fabric of marvels folded
down to a little space.

At our last meeting I closed
the ward door of heavy glass
between us, and saw your face
crumple, fine threadbare linen

worn, still good to the last,
then, somehow, smooth to a smile
so I should not see your tears.
Anguish: remembered hours:

a lamp on embroidered linen,
my supper set out, your voice
calling me in as darkness
falls on my father's house.

1981

Andante

New houses grasp our hillside,
my favourite walks are fenced.
Still there's the foreshore, still
transparent overlappings
seaward, let there be space
for the demon's timeless patience
with myself and my dying.

Silence fixes our loves.
Let me cultivate silence.
What's my head but a rat's nest
of dubious texts? Let water
ask me, what have you learned?
I tell the plush deeps, nothing.
Nightfall, an old vexed hour.

Why do I have an image
of owls with silver bells
hung from the tarsus, hunting
fieldmice round the new houses?
Hunger, music and death.
And after that the calm
full frontal stare of silence.

1981

A Welcome: Flowers and Fowls

Field of the cloth of gold!
Random as stars, the dandelions
crowd in their constellations.

A day of muted brightness
but for these blazing flowers
through which, at first by ones

and twos, then all at once,
a friendly host comes running.
Two beauties walk together,

Moorish princesses, distant
from the common flock; a few
are glossed in autumn colours,

bronze, sepia, russet brown.
All gather close and turn
their sharp archaic profiles —

You should have come with gifts
to us of ancient lineage.
We scratched the dust of Egypt.

Caesar carried us north.
We voyaged with Columbus.
I walk on, empty-handed

through taller reeds and grasses.
'O happy living things' —
as Coleridge says, the heart

must bless them, to be blessed.
And when at last I leave,
the flock, in benediction,

waits in the field of gold.
Seed of the seed of grasses
they fossick in will flourish.

Beyond the net of language
they know themselves immortal
as grassblade and grasshopper,

as the gods who fill their dishes.

1988

The Twins

Three years old when their mother died
in what my grandmother called
accouchement, my father labour,
they heard the neighbours intone
'A mercy the child went with her.'

Their father raised them somehow.
No one could tell them apart.
At seven they sat in school
in their rightful place, at the top
of the class, the first to respond
with raised arm and finger-flick.

When one gave the answer, her sister
repeated it under her breath.
An inspector accused them of cheating,
but later, in front of the class,
declared himself sorry, and taught us
a marvellous word: *telepathic*.

On Fridays, the story went,
they slept in the shed, barred in
from their father's rage as he drank
his dead wife back to his house.
For the rest of the week he was sober
and proud. My grandmother gave them
a basket of fruit. He returned it.
'We manage. We don't need help.'

They could wash their own hair, skin rabbits,
milk the cow, make porridge, clean boots.

Unlike most of the class I had shoes,
clean handkerchiefs, ribbons, a toothbrush.
We all shared the schoolsores and nits
and the language I learned to forget
at the gate of my welcoming home.

One day as I sat on the fence
my pinafore goffered, my hair
still crisp from the curlers, the twins
came by. I scuttled away
so I should not have to share
my Saturday sweets. My mother
saw me, and slapped me, and offered
the bag to the twins, who replied
one aloud and one sotto voce,
'No thank you. We don't like lollies.'

They lied in their greenish teeth
as they knew, and we knew.
                          Good angel
give me that morning again
and let me share, and spare me
the shame of my parents' rebuke.

If there are multiple worlds
then let there be one with an ending
quite other than theirs: leaving school
too early and coming to grief.

Or if this is our one life sentence,
hold them in innocence, writing
Our Father which art in Heaven
in copperplate, or drawing
(their work being done) the same picture
on the backs of their slates: a foursquare
house where a smiling woman
winged like an angel welcomes
two children home from school.

1988

Oodgeroo Noonuccal

b 1920, Stradbroke Island, south-eastern Queensland, and lives there; of the Noonuccal people; formerly known as Kath Walker. She has been influential in raising awareness of Aboriginal rights and culture. *My People* (1970).

We are Going

for Grannie Coolwell

They came in to the little town
A semi-naked band subdued and silent,
All that remained of their tribe.
They came here to the place of their old bora ground
Where now the many white men hurry about like ants.
Notice of estate agent reads: 'Rubbish May Be Tipped Here'.
Now it half covers the traces of the old bora ring.
They sit and are confused, they cannot say their thoughts:
'We are as strangers here now, but the white tribe are the strangers.
We belong here, we are of the old ways.
We are the corroboree and the bora ground,
We are the old sacred ceremonies, the laws of the elders.
We are the wonder tales of Dream Time, the tribal legends told.
We are the past, the hunts and the laughing games, the wandering camp fires.
We are the lightning-bolt over Gaphembah Hill
Quick and terrible,
And the Thunder after him, that loud fellow.
We are the quiet daybreak paling the dark lagoon.
We are the shadow-ghosts creeping back as the camp fires burn low.
We are nature and the past, all the old ways
Gone now and scattered.
The scrubs are gone, the hunting and the laughter.
The eagle is gone, the emu and the kangaroo are gone from this place.
The bora ring is gone.
The corroboree is gone.
And we are going.'

1964

No More Boomerang

No more boomerang
No more spear;
Now all civilized —
Colour bar and beer.

No more corroboree,
Gay dance and din.

Now we got movies,
And pay to go in.

No more sharing
What the hunter brings.
Now we work for money,
Then pay it back for things.

Now we track bosses
To catch a few bob,
Now we go walkabout
On bus to the job.

One time naked,
Who never knew shame;
Now we put clothes on
To hide whatsaname.

No more gunya,
Now bungalow,
Paid by higher purchase
In twenty year or so.

Lay down the stone axe,
Take up the steel,
And work like a nigger
For a white man meal.

No more firesticks
That made the whites scoff.
Now all electric,
And no better off.

Bunyip he finish,
Now got instead
White fella Bunyip,
Call him Red.

Abstract picture now —
What they coming at?
Cripes, in our caves we
Did better than that.

Black hunted wallaby,
White hunt dollar;
White fella witch-doctor
Wear dog-collar.

No more message-stick;
Lubras and lads
Got television now,
Mostly ads.

Lay down the woomera,
Lay down the waddy.
Now we got atom-bomb,
End *every*body.

1966

Gifts

'I will bring you love,' said the young lover,
'A glad light to dance in your dark eye.
Pendants I will bring of the white bone,
And gay parrot feathers to deck your hair.'

But she only shook her head.

'I will put a child in your arms,' he said,
'Will be a great headman, great rain-maker.
I will make remembered songs about you
That all the tribes in all the wandering camps
Will sing for ever.'

But she was not impressed.

'I will bring you the still moonlight on the lagoon,
And steal for you the singing of all the birds;
I will bring down the stars of heaven to you,
And put the bright rainbow into your hand.'

'No,' she said, 'bring me tree-grubs.'

1966

Dimitris Tsaloumas

b 1921, island of Leros, Greece; arrived in Australia 1952. He has taught in secondary schools, and lives in Melbourne. His poetry in Greek is published in Greece and Australia. *The Observatory* (1983), *Falcon Drinking* (1988).

Prodigal

Fanatical mosquitoes and persistent fetid stench
    hold absolute dominion
over the twilight swamps. Evening comes early
    full of mutterings. Our days
were never rich — but now!
    The ox is skin and bone and the goat
barely yields enough for the baby. Therefore
    make no rash decision.
The other day Eros was seen in the market-place
    unrecognized in cast-off clothes,
grown old. Come of course since you insist, but
    whatever you remember, now forget.

1983

The Return

The war's been over now for forty years
and you've still to take the enemy off the wire.
Who opened up his back so that his lungs hung out
from behind? Haven't you tired of his shallow screams
in a whole lifetime? I sent you word to empty out
the bucket with the arm and other bits,
to stop up all the cracks. The house
stinks like a shambles. You haven't even sealed
the holes in the cellar and who knows what
might suddenly creep out on us? I don't like
this weather at all. Already my sleep is taking
water, and there are tentacles stretching out,
feeling in the dark. I'm sorry to tell you,
brother, but I'm not spending summer here.
At our age some caution is called for.

1983

The first four poems here by Dimitris Tsaloumas were translated from the original Greek by Philip Grundy, assisted by the poet. 'Epilogue' was written in English.

Message

Green Cape, New South Wales

Tell her that I've made up my mind today that I
   shall never die. They've cut a path
without a past in the hallucinations of captivity
   and I thrust through the thickets of birdsong
and embroideries of light with the guileless snake
   right to the heart of immortality,
I saw the wild duck beak strained forward
   beating through the narrows of the ravine
and the hawk beautiful amid the frenzied squawks
   rising deadly scaling
the slopes of heaven. Tell her that her son
   came down to the spray-misted headlands
of the South and saw the onslaught of waves
   huge as island hills and cried out
The sea! The sea! And tell her that he changed his mind.
   She wasn't mean-spirited. She'll understand.

1983

Postponement

Where did I study, you ask — to send your son there too.
I've thought about it and I'll tell you,
but first let him go to a school with teachers.

1985

Epilogue

My joys are those of the spare autumn birds
that haunt the trees of sunset cities.

My sadness is in the patient eye of the ox,
the vast lament of the ass in night paddocks.

I claw and peck and bristle at competition
like a pink-stalked gull, and my greed

is infinite, though I loathe my brother the pig.
My lust is the lust of the goat who spies

the bare-breasted tourist on the rock
and shakes his beard with rage and climbs

down the bluff to take a sniff at the brine.
Only my thoughts are human, but I look

for alternatives. They bring me too close
to you, old friends; my perspective suffers.

1988

Geoffrey Dutton

b 1922, Anlaby Station, Kapunda, SA. After teaching English at the University of Adelaide 1953-62, he worked in Adelaide as a freelance writer, editor, arts administrator and novelist. He lives in Mudgee, central NSW. *A Body of Words* (1977), *Selective Affinities* (1985).

Comfort

[from *A Body of Words*]

No need to go further than 1601,
Thomas Campion's *A Book of Airs*,
'But when we come where comfort is, she never will say no.'

Not meaning a great bed, mirrors in the ceiling,
A blindfolded player on the viol d'amore,
Or even honey to be licked from her navel,
Simply 'Solace 1400', 'Pleasure, delight 1568.'
She'll soon tell him if she's uncomfortable,
Ants and thorns being the first enemies of love.

But beware! Don't believe in Sense 4:
'The condition or quality of being COMFORTABLE 1814.'
She is pagan or medieval, and this
Is leading straight to Victoria and Albert.
A loose, easy fit may do for old shoes,
Even for golden weddings, but not for lovers.

The noun 'love' waits on two active verbs,
And so comfort is not an ointment
That she rubs into the itch of his self-pity,
(If so, they would not be lovers),
But a liquor they drink together,
Distilled from that sturdy Latin, 'Strength together',
'To encourage, to invigorate 1674.'

She is right to refuse to be a soft consoler,
She is right to roll pleasure and strength together
And refuse to be 'A thing
That ministers to enjoyment and content 1659.'

But watch her when she is laughing, how wonderfully
She manages 'to cheer 1612',
And when a rock explodes in the fire,
And the hot blood is running down his cheek,
How she is all woman, the source of all comfort,
The one from whom weak strength was born.

1977

Love and Complacency

At Christmas, sometimes, even for unbelievers,
Angels come slanting down across the firebreak
Over flecks of summer grass on the sheep-tracked hill.
Dragonflies mirrored in the dam, weavers
Of transparencies, gyrate
Cerulean and ruby images of free will.

Dipping, drifting, they couple in mid-air
Like helicopters refuelling, carrying on
Mutual flirtations with the bronze face
Of the deep dam, their fuselages clear
As noon sky in the desert, or the red clarion
Venus sometimes flashes through black space.

They float through the branches of the mirrored trees.
A trout rises. They cross the concentric rings,
Wings transparent as angels', though the treasure
Of sex ballasts their jewelled bodies.
They brush the water's gum-blossoms with their wings.
The trout leaps. At least they died for pleasure.

1985

Nancy Keesing

b 1923, Sydney, and lives there. A former social worker, she has worked as an editor, arts administrator and freelance writer. *Hails and Farewells* (1977).

Olympus

One hundred and eighty degrees is the view from up there.
The windows are hooded, as eagles hood their eyes,
to shield the gods in colloquy from glare.

The boardroom table is wired for sound because
some gods are ageing and don't hear terribly well,
and some of them, after lunch, do nod and drowse.

Being born at the end of an era of hassock and steeple
I used to marvel that the Greeks, who invented reason,
could worship those commonplace Olympian people.

And here I am! The time is a quarter to one.
Amiable Zeus says: 'Ten minutes more, then lunch.'
Lovely Athena, wise in her Parthenon,

classic in logic, sums up the morning prayer:
petitions accepted, dismissed. Through all its degrees
how distant, yet sparkling close, is the view from up here.

1977

Old Hardware Store, Melbourne

Being un-organic, non-macrobiotic, lazy
I do not wish to return to the honest names
Or the slow, outmoded, heavy, intractable objects
As: mincers, mangles, mowers, mattocks, hames;
Collars and saddles of horsehair-padded leather;
Pots of cast and enamelled iron; hones
For sharpening blades of shares, shears, scythes and sickles;
Hafted axes; burrs and grinding stones.
    But I value verbs: to mill, till, harrow, harvest, burnish,
Hew, strip, beat, toss, tether, render, comb,
Roast, brew, knead, prove dough — one returns to bread,
To meat, to bellies and bowels, to prick and womb —
To bear, be born, to suck, piss, shit, to cry,
To work, sweat, live, sing, love, pray, die.

1977

Dorothy Hewett

b 1923, Perth; grew up on a farm at Wickepin, south-eastern WA. She taught English for a time at the University of WA, but most of her adult life has been spent in Sydney. She is also a noted playwright. *Rapunzel in Suburbia* (1975), *Alice in Wormland* (1987).

In Moncur Street

It's twenty years ago and more
since first I came to Moncur Street,
and lived with Aime and Alf among
the boarders on the second floor.

The stew was burnt, the budgie sang,
as Aime walked home the church-bells rang,

she banged the pots, ring-ding-a-ding,
she'd lost at Housie in the Spring.

But Sammy Smiles (that lovely man),
still visits her on Saturday,
Beat runs a book, and little Fay
whines in the stairwell every day
     in Moncur Street
     in Moncur Street.

Alf rose before the morning light,
and took a chopper in his hand;
he chopped and chopped in Oxford Street.
'Alf runs around without his head,
he's like a chook,' said Aime
     and sighed
for Sammy Smiles (that lovely man),

and Sunny Corner where she played
at 'Ladies' in the willow's shade.
At sunset by the empty shops
they swapped their dusty acid drops:
who lounges in the crystal air,
but Sammy Smiles, with marcelled hair!

I woke up in the darkest night,
knew all the world had caught alight.
The surf was pounding in the weather,
and Moncur Street was mine forever.
The little bat upon the stair
came out and flapped: it wasn't there,

the snapshot album turned and turned,
the stew caught fire, the budgie burned,
the pensioners at drafts and dreams,
picked bugs between their trouser seams.

And Sammy Smiles (that lovely man!)
and Aime and Alf and little Fay,
and Beat and Bert and betting slips,
the man I loved, the child I bore,
have all gone under Bondi's hills,
and will return here nevermore,
     in Moncur Street
     in Moncur Street.

Alf starts up his steady snore,
'Them Bondi sandhill's paved with gold,
I could've bought them for a song.'

The home brew bursts behind the door.
Aime lies upon her back and sighs:
'In Sunny Corner by the store
Sam kissed me once when I turned four.'

Dreams are deep and love is long:
she turns upon her other side.

1975

Grave Fairytale

I sat in my tower, the seasons whirled,
the sky changed, the river grew
and dwindled to a pool.
The black Witch, light as an eel,
laddered up my hair
to straddle the window-sill.

She was there when I woke, blocking the light,
or in the night, humming, trying on my clothes.
I grew accustomed to her; she was as much a part of me
as my own self; sometimes I thought, 'she *is* myself!'
a posturing blackness, savage as a cuckoo.

There was no mirror in the tower.

Each time the voice screamed from the thorny garden
I'd rise and pensively undo the coil,
I felt it switch the ground, the earth tugged at it,
once it returned to me knotted with dead warm birds,
once wrapped itself three times around the tower —
                              the tower quaked.
Framed in the window, whirling the countryside
with my great net of hair I'd catch a hawk,
                              a bird, and once a bear.
One night I woke, the horse pawed at the walls,
the cell was full of light, all my stone house
suffused, the voice called from the calm white garden,
                              'Rapunzel'.
I leant across the sill, my plait hissed out
                              and spun like hail;
he climbed, slow as a heartbeat, up the stony side,
we dropped together as he loosed my hair,
his foraging hands tore me from neck to heels:
the witch jumped up my back and beat me to the wall.

Crouched in a corner I perceived it all,
the thighs jack-knifed apart, the dangling sword
                              thrust home,

pinned like a specimen — to scream with joy.
I watched all night the beasts unsatisfied
roll in their sweat, their guttural cries
made the night thick with sound.
Their shadows gambolled, hunch-backed, hairy-arsed,
and as she ran four-pawed across the light,
the female dropped coined blood spots on the floor.

When morning came he put his armour on,
kissing farewell like angels swung on hair.
I heard the metal shoes trample the round earth
about my tower.
Three times I lent my hair to the glowing prince,
hand over hand he climbed, my roots ached,
the blood dribbled on the stone sill.
Each time I saw the framed-faced bully boy
sick with his triumph.

The third time I hid the shears,
a stab of black ice dripping in my dress.
He rose, his armour glistened in my tears,
the convex scissors snapped,
the glittering coil hissed, and slipped
through air to undergrowth.
His mouth, like a round O, gaped at his end,
his finger nails ripped out, he clawed through space.
His horse ran off flank-deep in blown thistles.
Three seasons he stank at the tower's base.
A hawk plucked out his eyes, the ants busied his brain,
the mud-weed filled his mouth, his great sword rotted,
his tattered flesh-flags hung on bushes for the birds.

Bald as a collaborator I sit walled
in the thumb-nosed tower,
wound round three times with ropes of autumn leaves.
And the witch . . . sometimes I idly kick
a little heap of rags across the floor.
I notice it grows smaller every year.

1975

Anniversary

Death is in the air —

today is the anniversary of his death in October
(he would have been thirty-one)
I went home to High Street
& couldn't feed the new baby

my milk had dried up
so I sat holding him numbly
looking for the soft spot on the top of his head
while they fed me three more librium
you're only crying for yourself he said
but I kept on saying *It's the waste I can't bear.*

All that winter we lived
in the longest street in the world
he used to walk to work in the dark
on the opposite side of the street
somebody always walked with him but they never met
he could only hear the boots
& when he stopped they stopped.

The new baby swayed in a canvas cot lacing his fingers
I worried in case he got curvature of the spine
Truby King said a baby needed firm support
he was a very big bright baby
the cleaner at the Queen Vic. said every morning
you mark my words that kid's been here before.

The house was bare & cold with a false gable
we had no furniture only a double mattress
on the floor a big table & two deal chairs
every morning I dressed the baby in a shrunken jacket
& caught the bus home to my mother's to nurse the child
who was dying   the house had bay windows
hidden under fir trees smothered in yellow roses
the child sat dwarfed at the end of the polished table
pale as death in the light of his four candles
singing *Little Boy Blue.*

I pushed the pram to the telephone box
I'm losing my milk I told her *I want to bring him
home to die   Home* she said *you left
home a long time ago to go with that man.*

I pushed them both through the park
over the dropped leaves (his legs were crippled)
a magpie swooped down black out of the sky
& pecked his forehead   a drop of blood splashed on
his wrist   he started to cry

It took five months & everybody was angry
because the new baby was alive & cried for attention
pollen sprinkled his cheeks under the yellow roses.

When he died it was like everybody else
in the public ward with the screens around him
the big bruises spreading on his skin
his hand came up out of the sheets *don't cry*
he said *don't be sad*

I sat there overweight in my Woolworth's dress
not telling anybody in case they kept him alive
with another transfusion —

    Afterwards I sat by the gas fire
in my old dressing gown turning over the photographs
wondering why I'd drunk all that stout
& massaged my breasts every morning to be
    a good mother.

           1979

Isobel Robin

b 1924, Sydney; has lived in Melbourne since 1939. She has worked as an advertising copywriter and as a secretary. *Pen Friends* (with Nan Bowman, 1984).

Freud's Back-yard

    Berggasse IX, Vienna

The doctor's not at home.
For a few schillings you may stroll
past letters, photos, musty souvenirs,
and old confessions
sheened like wax on weighty chairs
(though the body imprint's gone).

Prim, sequential, why do rooms like these
bring on uneasiness?
You find you're listening for dead people's pain.
Perhaps the wallpaper
covers too many secrets, old and mousey,
muttering where they scratch with dingy claws.

Go now, unnoticed — leave discreetly
through the door, then run —
follow your footsteps' echo
down cold stairs.

A dusty window, quaintly scrolled,
exposes Freud's back-yard:
a glimpse of shattered psyches spilling from a bin;
libido bagged for burial;
Oedipus howling for his Mum —

all in the mind!
There's no detritus here from dreadful dreams;
the sanely waltzing Viennese
have whipped it stiff and baked it in a torte.

[1986]

Frogs' Eggs

Uniformed for a Ladies' College —
Nine-year-olds, bemused by knowledge
When all that we really craved to know
Was 'Where did I come from? Where do I go?
What makes babies? And how? And why?'
And 'Thora Dawkin has swallowed a fly.
Is she going to die?'

Miss McRory, maiden lady,
Stout, black brogues and an eerie, shady
Green straw hat on her flame-hot bun,
Pursed her face against the sun,
Flexed her corset to ease exertion
And marched us on a nature excursion.

Later, at the tadpole creek
She let us paddle, gather, seek
In cool, wet eddies on cool, pale stones,
Slime in our toes and joy in our bones
And a century sun that withered the sky.
While Thora, who had swallowed a fly,
Could sicken and die.

Tadpoles flicked between our legs,
Squirmy, spermy, fruit of eggs;
In still, dark pools near mossy logs
Lay spotted jelly, promised frogs.
Vestigial truths from mysterious places
Stirred, untaught, across our faces.

Bulge-eyed frogs with catapult legs —
Amniotic sud of eggs
Already shaping tadpole tails —
Wine of Life in our jam-jar grails.

What made it start? And how? And why?
But Thora Dawkin, unwilling to die,
Disgorged her fly.

The long march back — a furnace mile
In giggling, straggling crocodile;
Miss McRory, forty, queasy,
Wondering why she felt uneasy
On currents of innocent, pristine glee,
That summer of nineteen-thirty-three.

Puritan school-ma'am, rest in peace
For answers come when the questions cease.
Those summer-wondering, pre-pubescent
Waders in waters of evanescent
Ignorance, learned how and why;
And time has fed us on many a fly
But we didn't all die.

[1988]

Francis Webb

1925-73; b Adelaide; educated in Sydney. As a young man he lived for some twelve years in Canada and UK. Diagnosed as schizophrenic, he spent much of his last twenty years in psychiatric hospitals. *Selected Poems* (1991).

Harry

[from *Ward Two*]

It's the day for writing that letter, if one is able,
And so the striped institutional shirt is wedged
Between this holy holy chair and table.
He has purloined paper, he has begged and cadged
The bent institutional pen,
The ink. And our droll old men
Are darting constantly where he weaves his sacrament.

Sacrifice? Propitiation? All are blent
In the moron's painstaking fingers — so painstaking.
His vestments our giddy yarns of the firmament,
Women, gods, electric trains, and our remaking
Of all known worlds — but not yet
Has our giddy alphabet
Perplexed his priestcraft and spilled the cruet of innocence.

We have been plucked from the world of commonsense,
Fondling between our hands some shining loot,
Wife, mother, beach, fisticuffs, eloquence,
As the lank tree cherishes every distorted shoot.
What queer shards we could steal
Shaped him, realer than the Real:
But it is no goddess of ours guiding the fingers and the thumb.

She cries: *Ab aeterno ordinata sum.*
He writes to the woman, this lad who will never marry.
One vowel and the thousand laborious serifs will come
To this pudgy Christ, and the old shape of Mary.
Before seasonal pelts and the thin
Soft tactile underskin
Of air were stretched across earth, they have sported and are one.

Was it then at this altar-stone the mind was begun?
The image besieges our Troy. Consider the sick
Convulsions of movement, and the featureless baldy sun
Insensible — sparing that compulsive nervous tic.
Before life, the fantastic succession,
An imbecile makes his confession,
Is filled with the Word unwritten, has almost genuflected.

Because the wise world has for ever and ever rejected
Him and because your children would scream at the sight
Of his mongol mouth stained with food, he has resurrected
The spontaneous thought retarded and infantile Light.
Transfigured with him we stand
Among walls of the no-man's-land
While he licks the soiled envelope with lover's caress

Directing it to the House of no known address.

1964

A Man

[from *Ward Two*]

He can hardly walk these days, buckling at the knees,
Wrestling with consonants, in raggedy khakis
Faded from ancient solar festivities,
He loiters, shuffles, fingering solid wall:
    Away down, the roots, away down,
    Who said Let there be light?

The clock in its tower of worked baroque stone
Holds at three o'clock and has always done.
Nothing else shuffles, works, is ended, begun,
There is only the solid air, the solid wall.
   Away down, the roots, away down,
   Who said Let there be light?

Three weeks under the indigent paid-off clock:
He pulls from his photograph album the heavy chock,
Squats like a king behind a heavy lock,
Niched in and almost part of solid wall.
   Away down, the roots, away down,
   Who said Let there be light?

Canaries silent as spiders, caged in laws,
Shuffle and teeter, begging a First Cause
That they may tear It open with their claws
And have It hanging in pain from solid wall.
   Away down, the roots, away down,
   Who said Let there be light?

His King's Cup for swimming, the shimmering girl,
The photogenic light aircraft spin and whirl
Out of the loam, stained by all weathers, hurl
Their petty weight against a solid wall.
   Away down, the roots, away down,
   Who said Let there be light?

The great goldfish hangs mouthing his glass box
And élite of weeds, like an old cunning fox
Or red-bronze gadfly, hangs in contentment, mocks
All that is cast in air or solid wall.
   Away down, the roots, away down,
   Who said Let there be light?

But his Cup glitters, the light monoplane bucks
Into the head-wind, girls in panel trucks
Arrive like flowers, and the dry mouth sucks
Deeply, puffs into flesh behind solid wall.
   Away down, the roots, away down,
   Who said Let there be light?

1964

Nessun Dorma

(in memory of Jussi Björling)

Past six o'clock. I have prayed. No one is sleeping.
I have wandered past the old maternity home's
Red stone fermented by centuries; and there comes
New light, new light; and the cries of the rooks sweeping
To their great nests are guerilla light in a fusion
— Murmurs, echoes, plainsong; and the night
Will be all an abyss and depth of light between
Two shorelines in labour: birth and death. O passion
(One light in the hospital window) of quickening light,
O foetus quaking towards light, sound the gaunt green,
Trawl Norfolk, and make shiver the window-blind,
Harass nebulae for Björling. Find him, find.

And now the bar, the feeble light, glissade
Of tables and glasses, and the mantel-set
Intoning his death. Broad tender sunlights fret
Our twilight, his remembered voice has laid
Cock-crow and noon upon harrowed palms of the sill.
O broad light and tender, lucent aria,
Lacerate my paling cheeklines with the steep
Bequest of light and tears, flood me until
The man is the dawning child; be anathema
To man-made darkness. No one, no one shall sleep
Till the cry of the infant emergent, lost and lame,
Is the cry of a death gone towering towards the Flame.

1967

Lament for St Maria Goretti

Six o'clock. The virginal belly of a screen
Winces before the blade, the evening wind:
Diluted, a star
Twitches like a puddle on scoured hygienic stone.
All of the documents signed and countersigned
And truce to a cruel war:

Nessun Dorma: 'None shall sleep', an aria in *Turandot* by Puccini. *Jussi Björling*: Swedish tenor (1911-60). *Norfolk*: Webb stayed for a time in Norfolk, in the UK.

Lament for St Maria Goretti: Maria Goretti (1890-1902) was a child canonized as a martyr for Christian life, who died of stab wounds after resisting rape. She survived for 24 hours, with a family friend, Teresa Cimarelli, watching by her bed in the hospital at Nettuno, near Anzio. She had lived in deep poverty with her family at Ferriere, in the Pontine marshes, where her father died when she was ten. Corinaldo, near Ancona, is the place of her early happy childhood. Angelino was a younger brother. The Angelus is a prayer to the virgin Mary, traditionally made at the ringing of churchbells at 6 a.m., noon and 6 p.m.

Wreckage gesticulates, toothless broken ships,
Meteorite, cherubim, Horseman, in the wash of space
Round the petty bays of this child's face.

Teresa, it is easier now. But the chloroform
Comes like a stiletto to our gasping void:
Sometimes you look lovely swimming there beside me
While chloroform unravels the holy lines of your face,
I would take you into my hands to remould you, shape you,
But the pain, the pain . . .
                          See Teresa, my father Luigi is coming
Out of the cemetery (but the chloroform holds) shouldering away
The earth. He touches his little Cross with his lips,
I am crying, and a flight of birds hangs like a rosary,
He is smiling, but the chloroform will dissolve him . . .

Six o'clock. The bells of Nettuno chime
Angelus: Ave to Ave, hand to hand
The buckets of sound are passed in a slow time
Up to a thirsting land.
Again the breeze at the hospital window flutters in lace
Near the thirsting wilderness of this child's face.

Touch me, Teresa: you know you often asked me
Why I was in tears at Mass before the Communion:
I seemed to see Him there, heaving up to Golgotha,
And rising and falling. I stood there mocking Him
Like when I stole two spoonfuls of Angelino's polenta
(You haven't committed a sin, said the kind old priest):
Three times He fell: the last note of the Angelus
Falls with Him — I am falling with Him
— Must I fall with Him into chloroform?
Take up your cross. Touch me. Teresa, quickly . . .

Six o'clock. There may be a moon tonight.
At dead Ferriere twitches the comatose star.
A peasant knows the early mosquito bite
Like a stiletto into his wincing ear.
The suave impersonal light
Trails its skirts over marshland: no mourners here,
And Nothing mourns at Nettuno: feel the embrace
Of Nothing scrambling ashore at this child's face.

Teresa, he's coming: *don't, you will go to Hell* . . .
Teresa, I can still see you: Ferriere is closing in:
The chloroform works at you. Be dainty Corinaldo
Where I was born. I can hardly read or write:

But your breast is our little pet hill, your hair like shadows
Of clouds on our grain, your mouth like a watercourse.
Have you spoken? have words of water been truly uttered
To my thirst — it's this drumming, drumming in my ears.
Teresa, I am going. Teresa, to the last be Corinaldo,
All life writing me on earth:
Let my hands reach you — I can hardly sign my name:
My signature, my scrawl: no wait, Teresa, Teresa . . .

Six o'clock. And the Miserere. Final Grace.
And Death and the Woman, strangely at one, will place
Ambiguous fingers on all of this child's face.

1977

Vincent Buckley

1925–89; b Romsey, central Victoria, of Irish parents. Also an influential critic, he taught English at the University of Melbourne. *Selected Poems* (1981).

No New Thing

No new thing under the sun:
The virtuous who prefer the dark;
Fools knighted; the brave undone;
The athletes at their killing work;
The tender-hearts who step in blood;
The sensitive paralysed in a mood;
The clerks who rubber-stamp our deaths,
Executors of death's estate;
Poets who count their dying breaths;
Lovers who pledge undying hate;
The self-made and self-ruined men;
The envious with the strength of ten.

They crowd in nightmares to my side,
Enlisting even private pain
In some world-plan of suicide:
Man, gutted and obedient man,
Who turns his coat when he is told,
Faithless to our shining world.
And hard-faced men, who beat the drum
To call me to this Cause or that,
Those heirs of someone else's tomb,
Can't see the sweeter work I'm at,
The building of the honeycomb.

1966

from *Golden Builders*

VII

With the spring rains, small spiders
weave themselves into the walls
till now this one   unravelling his body
climbs in a long curve floorward
towards undizzied stillness.

                      As I towards sleep.

Seconal   the sweet bubble
comes and goes in the mouth
dying for a cigarette.

So then   the nightmares
I am rolled in sleep   am I
free?   free to mean
something of my own?   The limewhite faces
lower at each other
as if shorn from bodies. The feet in the dance
slowing down.   At what speed
how deep
down does the mind
just disappear   and in its turn
be dreamed   its lingering?
                  Once
I went out into the cold mist,
two figures dragging the third body
into the lane. I cried out   I put out my hand
madly   fingers like a grille.
There was no lane, no bodies.

The brain collapsing into stillness
voices decomposing in too much space
hills filling with slow white sound
the computer skating on the wrong name

                  In sleep you go
back up into the old brain
wound tightly as the old city,
walled, thirsty, alive.   Come out
as from a seance   to the choke of white bread
the rubbed taste in your mouth
bones standing up
in the water of your face.

Golden Builders: a poem in 27 sections, which meditates on existence in inner-urban Carlton and Fitzroy in Melbourne.

                    Every morning
eyes staring backward
into the skull, trying to recall it,
I hear the chop and change of the machines.

VIII

Timid and hot-tempered
all his years in South Brunswick
my uncle swaggered like a rentier,
never got to know
the city too carnal for him.
In forty years my aunt had never seen him
wholly undressed. He brushed his foxy hair
sideways on his skull, walked
from the knees, with a camel's lope,
down all streets to the Sarah Sands
sickened for hillside air. Behind
the puzzled kindness of his face
swayed his hot dreams of decency.

IX   Fitzroy, Carlton

Even in the cemetery
where the crows and magpies
stood for hours on the bunched tops
of the few trees, they've put
flat green metal shields
like shock-troops
along the railings. The highrise flats
are guarded from the dead.

Who will guard me from the dead?

Vasko, Croat Socialist, sold me his typewriter
but couldn't bear to part. He stroked it
as he talked, and laughed. Needs the money,
and wants a friend to have it. So
a man may turn his goods into effects
while still alive.

                    And Roman, Ukrainian,
proud as a Turk,
practising honour in Fitzroy

Sarah Sands: a local pub.

as if he could stare up wheat
in Brunswick Street,
died at one corner, in the slimed oil
of his motorbike. And left his two best friends
to quarrel over his radiogram.
One flamboyant commanding
the other steady and furtive
both manoeuvring to impress me, unwilling
mediator.

        And Milan, counting his books
every day,
touching the spines before he would risk entering
the long sloping lines of his diary,
pacifist, dreaming of Brazil,
the words of friendship halting on his tongue.

In my country . . . my country . . . my country.
No mothers here. All deaths flat, metallic.

X   Micro-Biology I

Been here before. Through
the smart-arsed doors
two deep stairs lock. White coated demonstrators
carry their phials in front of them like tulips
and flick you with their eyes.

I've been up here before.
If you pause, just here,
halfway up the clanking stairway,
and lift your head, let your shoulders
feel them, listen at their feet

you can hear them, over and across the shallow ceiling,
the sixth floor, a floor of dogs

the sound of them
sifting out like blows; voices,
their one voice, the building
breathes them at every corner.

Think of them at the live bone
at the tender unpeeled wood
their voices crossing like the yelps of children;
think how, in any circumstances,
the body makes   will make its effort.

1976

Origins

Down the unreasonably humped
and winding back road, patriarch, he would carry
the week's supplies: whiskey,
bread, tea, jam,
the bushels of feed, the picture calendar,
maybe something to read
for the children: not the mother: not himself.

Through the two gates, with their old rusty
tin plaques, he was cut off
as in a highrock wilderness.

He kept no line to us; he never left
his name written; he rode, or walked,
the brown hills like a severed body.

So let you ease your mind back
inch by inch, as if prying
through the tiers of a history, back
to the closed soft place, with its must
of dark orderings, and dried rot,
from which, by a peculiar effort,
you might see, behind, pre-Celtic,
the clear air-shape of mountains.

Home   where your father gulped
the water and sugar
of a mother's love, and the whole house
kept its nap of smell
against the outdoors cold winds
and the earth-centred heat.

Rustle of sacks, the straw-ends
crushed in, the seasoned leather,
mice, spittle, bread, dung, oats,
whiskey, old papers, the sunsmell beating down
onto the halfdoor, from between round hills,
till it took a mushroom or a tuberous
density; smell of sapling in the ash.
In these smells we were begotten.

1979

Bruce Beaver

b 1928, Manly, Sydney, and lives there. He has had various manual and clerical occupations, and since the early 1960s has been a freelance journalist. *Selected Poems* (1991).

from *Letters to Live Poets*

X

The sou'wester whips the day awake.
The pines are tossing 'monkey tails'
about the gardens and the streets.
The air hums and rushes overhead
and next-door the little girl
is calling out to it.
All week she has blown
a two-note whistle and called the tune
her own. The white and blue weather
excites her. The wind blows
back into her face the tune.
She catches it and feels it blown
about her hair and face.
It buzzes like wild bees;
it stings with specks of dust and sand.
Yet over it and under it is the cool
to warmer charm of the September breeze,
spiked with salt and mellowed with
the mild juice of new grass.

The sheets crack and flap a semaphore
among the red and blue and black of 'coloureds'
She sits cross-legged beneath
the carousel of washing, fluting
and singing two notes, two words:
'I am, I am'. The mother
admonishes. She is thin and sallow,
without a man. Has her reasons
all about her like an angry
counterpoint. All winter
she has yelled at the child who yells
back at herself 'I am, I am'.
But the devas of the air and sky
respond 'We are, we are' and lift her
over the yards and the thrumming pines,
past gargling crows and creaking gulls,
above the splintering enamel
of the blue and whitening bay

back to where she is with a man
out of the clouds. The 'he' who'll spank
her mother good and bring them all
toffee apples every day.

How she sings and makes the whistle
talk with her. When she goes
inside the house her hair will crackle
and float about. Her mother will lick
the corner of a handkerchief
and clean the corners of her eyes.
Then by herself again
she'll clean the whistle's gritty mouth
and listen to it humming to
itself.
            Do you hear them now?
Have I admitted something past
my manhood? Do we recollect
blowing up a sunny storm
all by ourselves once upon
a time in a backyard garden
near the sea?
Or is it that all women
learn to sing to themselves early
that some men, early or late,
may listen?

                                                            1969

Machine

The bicycle on the balcony,
resplendently blue in the wan weather,
reclines in the cornice, the handlebars
horning over a thirty foot drop,
perched on by unbelievably gaudy
lorikeets whose slate pencil scratching
shrieks undo their beauty. The balcony
suffers the bicycle like a metal haemorrhoid
despite its angular attractiveness, its wiry
wheeled being of speed and jaunty games.
It does not beg to be straddled, to have
somebody bunching or cupping its bony
seat, it is in the best tradition of bachelor-
or spinster-dom. It stays alone and likes it.
So far this morning it has suffered the edges
of a storm and does not look wet or seem
ready to fantasise about rusting. Soon enough

someone will come and commandeer
its unforlorn integrity; will bounce and push it
down the felted concrete stairs and back into
the tacky tarsealed street of holes and bumps
where it will override indignity
and be itself admirably, elegantly.

1988

Peter Porter

b 1929, Brisbane. He has lived in London since 1951, at first working in advertising, and then as a freelance writer and critic. *A Porter Selected* (1989).

The Sadness of the Creatures

We live in a third floor flat
among gentle predators
and our food comes often
frozen but in its own shape
(for we hate euphemisms
as you would expect) and our cat's
food comes in tins, other than
scraps of the real thing and she
like a clever cat makes milk
of it for her kittens: we shout
of course but it's electric
like those phantom storms
in the tropics and we think of
the neighbours — I'm not writing
this to say how guilty
we are like some well-paid
theologian at an American
College on a lake
or even to congratulate
the greedy kittens who have
found their mittens and are up
to their eyes in pie — I know
lots of ways of upsetting
God's syllogisms, real
seminar-shakers some of them,
but I'm an historical cat
and I run on rails and so
I don't frame those little poems
which take three lines to
get under your feet —
you know the kind of thing —

The water I boiled the lobster in
is cool enough to top
up the chrysanthemums.
No, I'm acquisitive and have
one hundred and seven Bach
Cantatas at the last count,
but these are things of the spirit
and my wife and our children
and I are animals (biologically
speaking) which is how the world
talks to us, moving on the billiard
table of green London, the sun's
red eye and the cat's green eye
focussing for an end. I know
and you know and we all know
that the certain end of each of us
could be the end of all of us,
but if you asked me what
frightened me most, I wouldn't
say the total bang or even
the circling clot in the red drains
but the picture of a lit room
where two people not disposed
to quarrel have met so
oblique a slant of the dark
they can find no words for
their appalled hurt but only
ride the rearing greyness:
there is convalescence from this,
jokes and love and reassurance,
but never enough and never
convincing and when the cats
come brushing for food their soft
aggression is hateful;
the trees rob the earth and the earth
sucks the rain and the children
burgeon in a time of invalids —
it seems a trio sonata
is playing from a bullock's
skull and the God of Man
is born in a tub of entrails;
all man's regret is no more
than Attila with a cold
and no Saviour here or
in Science Fiction will come
without a Massacre of the Innocents
and a Rape of El Dorado.

1970

On First Looking into Chapman's Hesiod

For 5p at a village fête I bought
Old Homer-Lucan who popped Keats's eyes,
Print smaller than the Book of Common Prayer
But Swinburne at the front, whose judgement is
Always immaculate. I'll never read a tenth
Of it in what life I have left to me
But I did look at *The Georgics*, as he calls
The Works and Days, and there I saw, not quite
The view from Darien but something strange
And balking — Australia, my own country
And its edgy managers — in the picture of
Euboean husbandry, terse family feuds
And the minds of gods tangential to the earth.

Like a Taree smallholder splitting logs
And philosophizing on his dangling billies,
The poet mixes hard agrarian instances
With sour sucks to his brother. Chapman, too,
That perpetual motion poetry machine,
Grinds up the classics like bone meal from
The abattoirs. And the same blunt patriotism,
A long-winded, emphatic, kelpie yapping
About our land, our time, our fate, our strange
And singular way of moons and showers, lakes
Filling oddly — yes, Australians are Boeotians,
Hard as headlands, and, to be fair, with days
As robust as the Scythian wind on stone.

To teach your grandmother to suck eggs
Is a textbook possibility in New South Wales
Or outside Ascra. And such a genealogy too!
The Age of Iron is here, but oh the memories
Of Gold — pioneers preaching to the stringybarks,
Boring the land to death with verses and with
Mental Homes. 'Care-flying ease' and 'Gift-
Devouring kings' become the Sonata of the Shotgun
And Europe's Entropy; for 'the axle-tree, the quern,

On First Looking into Chapman's Hesiod: George Chapman (1559–1634) translated the early Greek poets Homer and Hesiod. Lucan (39–65) was a Roman of Spanish origin, whose epic poetry is considered inferior to earlier classics in the genre. *The Works and Days* by Hesiod describes life in his native Boeotia, a rural independent Greek state. Ascra was his birthplace. Euboea and Corinth were neighbouring Greek states, the former predominantly rural, the latter known for its urban sophistication. Helicon was a mountain in Boeotia, sacred to the muses. Scythia was a kingdom some hundreds of kilometres north-east, on the Black Sea. George Steiner is a contemporary critic of European literature, associated with Cambridge.

The hard, fate-fostered man' you choose among
The hand castrator, kerosene in honey tins
And mystic cattlemen: the Land of City States
Greets Australia in a farmer's gods.

Hesiod's father, caught in a miserable village,
Not helped by magic names like Helicon,
Sailed to improve his fortunes, and so did
All our fathers — in turn, their descendants
Lacked initiative, other than the doctors' daughters
Who tripped to England. Rough-nosed Hesiod
Was sure of his property to a slip-rail —
Had there been grants, he'd have farmed all
Summer and spent winter in Corinth
At the Creative Writing Class. Chapman, too,
Would vie with Steiner for the Pentecostal
Silver Tongue. Some of us feel at home nowhere,
Others in one generation fuse with the land.

I salute him then, the blunt old Greek whose way
Of life was as cunning as organic. His poet
Followers still make me feel déraciné
Within myself. One day they're on the campus,
The next in wide hats at a branding or
Sheep drenching, not actually performing
But looking the part and getting instances
For odes that bruise the blood. And history,
So interior a science it almost seems
Like true religion — who would have thought
Australia was the point of all that craft
Of politics in Europe? The apogee, it seems,
Is where your audience and its aspirations are.

'The colt, and mule, and horn-retorted steer' —
A good iambic line to paraphrase.
Long storms have blanched the million bones
Of the Aegean, and as many hurricanes
Will abrade the headstones of my native land:
Sparrows acclimatize but I still seek
The permanently upright city where
Speech is nature and plants conceive in pots,
Where one escapes from what one is and who
One was, where home is just a postmark
And country wisdom clings to calendars,
The opposite of a sunburned truth-teller's
World, haunted by precepts and the Pleiades.

1975

The Lying Art

It is all rhetoric rich as wedding cake
and promising the same bleak tears
when what was asked for but not recognized
shows its true face after a thousand breakfasts.

This, not Miss Moore's disclaimer, tells me
why I too dislike it. It is paid to distract us,
to tell the man disappointed by his mother
that he too can be a huge cry-baby.

Think of its habit of talking to gods
but saying only pastoral things. Real pain
it aims for, but can only make gestures,
the waste of selling-short, the 'glittering'.

I want you to be happy, you say,
but poetry brings in childhood on its horse,
the waves of parrots and the Delphic eyes,
and is never there when the scab is picked.

Music gets the better of it, since music is all lies.
Lies which fill the octave. Chromatic space
in verse turns out to be the ego's refractions,
truth always stained by observation.

So this argument goes in cut-up prose,
four lines to each part. I will not say
metric or stanzas or anything autonomous,
but keep to discontent, a nearly truthful art.

And what has this to do with poetry? Inroads
into rhetoric. The ugly and the disappointed
painting their faces with words; water showing
God's love to the beautiful — no way of changing.

Then we might as well make the best of
dishonesty, accept that all epithalamiums
are sugar and selfishness. Our world
of afterwards will have no need of lies.

1978

Miss Moore: Marianne Moore (1887-1972), American poet, whose poem 'Poetry' begins, 'I, too, dislike it'.

The Easiest Room in Hell

At the top of the stairs is a room
one may speak of only in parables.

It is the childhood attic,
the place to go when love has worn away,
the origin of the smell of self.

We came here on a clandestine visit
and in the full fire of indifference.

We sorted out books and let the children
sleep here away from creatures.

From its windows, ruled by willows,
the flatlands of childhood stretched
to the watermeadows.

It was the site of a massacre,
of the running down of the body
to less even than the soul,
the tribe's revenge on everything.

It was the heart of England
where the ballerinas were on points
and locums laughed through every evening.

Once it held all the games,
Inconsequences, Misalliance, Frustration,
even *Mendacity, Adultery* and *Manic Depression.*

But that was just its alibi,
all along it was home,
a home away from home.

Having such a sanctuary
we who parted here
will be reunited here.

You asked in an uncharacteristic note,
'Dwell I but in the suburbs
of your good pleasure?'

I replied, 'To us has been allowed
the easiest room in hell.'

Once it belonged to you,
now it is only mine.

1978

The Easiest Room in Hell: one of a series of poems written after the death of the poet's wife.

Bruce Dawe

b 1930, Geelong, Victoria. He worked in manual jobs in Victoria and spent nine years in the RAAF. Since 1972 he has taught English at what is now University College of Southern Queensland, Toowoomba. *Sometimes Gladness* (3rd edn, 1988).

The Not-so-good Earth

For a while there we had 25-inch Chinese peasant families
famishing in comfort on the 25-inch screen
and even Uncle Billy whose eyesight's going fast
by hunching up real close to the convex glass
could just about make them out — the riot scene
in the capital city for example
he saw that better than anything, using the contrast knob
to bring them up dark — all those screaming faces
and bodies going under the horses' hooves — he did a terrific job
on that bit, not so successful though
on the quieter parts where they're just starving away
digging for roots in the not-so-good earth
cooking up a mess of old clay
and coming out with all those Confucian analects
to everybody's considerable satisfaction
(if I remember rightly Grandmother dies
with naturally a suspenseful break in the action
for a full symphony orchestra plug for Craven A
neat as a whistle probably damn glad
to be quit of the whole gang with their marvellous patience).
We never did find out how it finished up . . . Dad
at this stage tripped over the main lead in the dark
hauling the whole set down smack on its inscrutable face,
wiping out in a blue flash and curlicue of smoke
600 million Chinese without a trace . . .

1968

The Raped Girl's Father

The buzz-saw whine of righteous anger rose
murderously in his throat throughout the night,
long after she had watched her mother close
the door to, and the honeyed wedge of light
was eaten by the dark, his voice whirred on,
and in that darker dark in which she lay
she felt his jaws rasp on the naked bone
of time and place and what she'd need to say
and how, if he were judge, by Christ, he'd cut . . .

She knew that glare of blindness that came down
upon him like a weather-wall and shut
him off from pity — hunched inside her gown
she shrank from what the morning held, the fresh assault
of reason that his manic shame would make,
the steady rape wished on her for her fault
in being the unlucky one to take
the fancy of another man who'd said:
'OK, this one will do . . . ' and swung the wheel.
Somebody sobbed. Grief mimed out in her head
the ritual she did not dare to feel.
Bones, she was dice-bones, shaken, rolled on black,
wishing her frenzied suitors might re-pass,
and at this stage be merciful, take her back,
and leave her, shuddering, blank-faced, on the grass.

1969

Homecoming

All day, day after day, they're bringing them home,
they're picking them up, those they can find, and bringing them home,
they're bringing them in, piled on the hulls of Grants, in trucks, in convoys,
they're zipping them up in green plastic bags,
they're tagging them now in Saigon, in the mortuary coolness
they're giving them names, they're rolling them out of
the deep-freeze lockers — on the tarmac at Tan Son Nhut
the noble jets are whining like hounds,
they are bringing them home
— curly-heads, kinky-hairs, crew-cuts, balding non-coms
— they're high, now, high and higher, over the land, the steaming *chow mein*
their shadows are tracing the blue curve of the Pacific
with sorrowful quick fingers, heading south, heading east,
home, home, home — and the coasts swing upward, the old ridiculous curvatures
of earth, the knuckled hills, the mangrove-swamps, the desert emptiness . . .
in their sterile housing they tilt towards these like skiers
— taxiing in, on the long runways, the howl of their homecoming rises
surrounding them like their last moments (the mash, the splendour)
then fading at length as they move
on to small towns where dogs in the frozen sunset
raise muzzles in mute salute,
and on to cities in whose wide web of suburbs
telegrams tremble like leaves from a wintering tree
and the spider grief swings in his bitter geometry
— they're bringing them home, now, too late, too early.

1969

Planning a Service

The folk from *Emoh Ruo* will be there,
and several budgies grousing away like senior citizens,
a couple of dogs with bright brown eyes,
a bunch of slatey-backs, feet nervously working,
some worms, some tattered moths, row after row
of ants, and, in the back pew a handful
of Christmas beetles lending a shy
iridescent charm to the congregation.
The Introit will be led by an irrepressible child,
the Credo intoned by the bees that live in the hive
in the base of the lilly-pilly near Norwood Street,
a special arrangement of the Alleluia will be rendered
by a squadron of maggies released from regular duties
dive-bombing the kids at Holy Name,
the Gospel will be John, of course, either 14 or 15,
read by a cricket, leaning well into the mike,
and then . . .
                    at the Consecration — at the Consecration I want
nothing, let the plain man, the centurion,
say it all, while for the Post-Communion
Beethoven's *Hymn to Joy* will be sung by a choir
of chooks of all ages redeemed from the broiler-house hell,
their wings extended, wattles and combs blood-red,
and finally, after the Blessing, please leave the church-door open,
in case a little wind, and a few leaves,
should sneak in out of the cold.

1983

The Sadness of Madonnas

on the famous news-photo of an Ethiopian mother and child

The sadness of madonnas is that they
at times too easily satisfy
our hunger for aesthetic balance, our deep craving
for harmony in hell — the eyes look sideways down,
pondering imponderable mysteries, such as where
the next meal's coming from, the robe
frayed at the edges frames the high-cheekboned face;
her grave full lips, if they could speak,
would utter (so we think) such other-worldly wisdom
as we're familiar with (suffering ennobles; this present
vale of tears is, after all, not *all*; He will not ask us
to bear above what we are able . . .)

---

centurion: see Luke 7:6–9.

Admittedly, the arms are far too thin
for comfort, bony fingers
framing the child's large skull
suggest the truth which plainly speaks
in the lustrous eyes, the xylophone
rib-cage and the wasted
music of leg-bones — such images
separate, and blur, and coalesce
in the terrible litany of particulars:
the thousands lying silent in the dirt,
the dehydrated children's skin as tough as leather,
the little fingers creeping out for comfort,
the grieving hearts that hold them . . .

1986

An Epiphany

O Life, you have your pearls beyond price palmed ready to delight us
when we least expect them!
                    For example, *this*:
the State Cabinet, newly-appointed, shining with the oils of chrism
— in this land where, through the mysterious divination of the ballot-box,
those who are first shall be deemed to be last, the lame and the halt
make it to the feast anyway on second preferences,
while he who is intelligent is startled by his inconsequence
— this marvellous assortment of the unseemly
appearing, as is the custom, on the second-floor balcony of Parliament House
to acknowledge the salutations and hosannas of the faithful gathered below,
are confounded to hear a voice, from the back of the crowd,
cry out with all the eccentricity of reason:
'JUMP! JUMP!'

1986

Evan Jones

b 1931, Melbourne. He taught English at the University of Melbourne 1963–89. *Recognitions* (1978), *Left at the Post* (1984).

The Point

for R.A. Simpson

The point, I imagine, is
not to learn to expect
betrayal, self-deceit, lies
however thick they collect
in the cul-de-sac of one's days,
half-noticed, half-numbered, half-checked:

but rather to learn to praise
fidelity, trust and love
which in their modest ways
continue to be and move
(however mocked, however derided,
however difficult, indeed, to prove),
utterly undivided —
if inarticulate or mute,
still mortally decided.

Neither fashionable nor astute
this point to take to heart:
merely final and absolute:

without it no people, no life, no art.

1978

Drinking with Friends

for Brian Buckley

We used to sit up until three or four
drinking whatever there was: the decor
was characteristically indiscriminate,
the company, those curious and articulate
about politics, art, psychology. It seemed
to me I stammered, others talked: I'm damned
if I can remember getting much of a hearing.
My friends remember me as domineering.

Sing hey, sing hey for those yesterdays,
the brilliant chat and its wanton ways,
lost, of course, in a golden haze.
It's nice to talk with old friends.

Commonly it's more comfortable now
with O.K. wines and breezier talk: somehow
things have increased and declined. But when the chatter
turns as it still will do to what things matter,
my helpless lack of dicta earns reproof:
haughty I'm thought, unamenable, aloof.
The only thing one never can imagine
is how one looks to others, with or without wine.

Sing ho, sing ho for the silences:
not one of us is as glib as he was
before the whiff of defeat gave him pause.
It's nice to talk with old friends.

1984

Poem just after midnight: summer: at home

for Leigh and Neta Astbury

For a moment, I heard the surge of waves
in the wind in the trees in my back-yard:
forty years collapsed for an instant.
Among my books and papers, secure
in a kind of reputation,
what takes my mind is wind, wind in the trees
and the vast rolling of water. When
my bones are washed quite white, who will
remember my patient efforts to mimic
in words the smaller rhythms
of private life with its rewards and frustrations?
Somebody might. It hardly seems to matter
as I listen again for the wind to toss the trees,
the whole stir of a world
moving away.

1984

Philip Martin

b 1931, Melbourne. He taught English at Monash University in Melbourne 1964–88, and has written and presented literary programmes on radio. He lives in Sydney. *New and Selected Poems* (1988).

Preserved

for Laila Haglund

The Falu copper-mine in central Sweden
Reaches back into prehistory,
And it's still working. Back some generations:
A young man wanders into passages
Long disused. Is lost. Then found years later:
Preserved, perfect, if a little brown.
'His fiancée,' a man says: 'She's still living.'
The old woman identifies the body.

§

Some winter days recall and promise spring.
And when spring comes, ice cracks and you see fish
Long sealed up, swimming.

Fifty years since I last saw this body!
They and the mine-breath
Have hardened it, and tanned it. Where is the spirit

That once sang in it, swore
'You are my song'? This shape I see is changed,
However 'like'. I tell these people 'Yes:

Yes, that's Sten.' (It's not, of course.) Then creak
Away, arthritic fingers at two sticks,
And my heart as if it were still

Twenty, and we strolled between the lakes,
Wild-strawberry-gathering, kissing them
Into each other's mouths.

Two bodies time has gripped, but differently.
And one with a soul still in it,
Ready to leap again. Old woman, girl.

What is this to me?

What do they expect me to say,
Or do? Burst into tears,
Break into flower?

This, once, was my lover.
My lover's body.
But the copper-salts

Have worked on it.
And time on me.
A mummy, and a mummied heart.

I feel nothing at all.

'Thank you,' I say. '*Thank* you.'

§

You find him for me now? The hour is late.

I grieved three years, then took another man.
He was a good husband, steady, gave me
Five children. And death has taken three,
Along with him. And now I'm free to marry.
Sten I never forgot. Not quite. I tried to,

Sten, pronounced *staen*, means stone.

Being a faithful wife. You bring him out
True to his name as never in his life.
What mockery. Free to marry stone.
The lips are bared to the clenched teeth. No voice,
Thank God no voice comes: 'Will you take me?'

I shall revolve all this till the breath goes.

§

I never married.
Nobody knew for certain where he'd got to.
I couldn't believe he'd left me,
Just gone off,
Nor that he was dead. He was too alive.
But the years, they left,
He never came. My family pestered me.
'You're a fine, healthy girl. Marry. Make babies.'
I slipped through their persuasions.
Slipped, too, with another man, who came
And went, and came
Back to the summer pillow of my breast.
I had no child, I couldn't have a child.
I'm glad. Glad to have lived
The way I did, and glad I'm almost done.
And now is the moment when you find me Sten:
'At least we *think* it's him.'
I look at the effigy. How absurd life is
To show me this when it's no use to me,
Let alone to itself.
You ask 'Is this Sten Lindgren?' So I cough
(I've a bad cough these days)
And fumble a little. 'Yes,' I tell you. 'And no.'
'Senile,' you don't quite say. Well, let it be.

1988

A Certain Love

There's no gainsaying this:
We're blessed. We know it.
And if God came to me today and said
'You must give her up', I'd answer
'Ridiculous. Why contradict yourself?'

1988

Kevin Gilbert

b 1933, Condobolin, central NSW; parentage part-white, part-Aboriginal, of the Wiradjuri people. He left school early, worked as a labourer and spent time in jail. Also a playwright, and a leading advocate of Aboriginal rights and culture, he lives in Canberra. *People Are Legends* (1978).

'Consultation'

Me, mate?
You'll get no views from me!
Where did I ever go?
Who did I ever meet?
What did I ever see?
Nothin' just the old river, the gumtree
The mission. Me seven kids, four grandkids
Blacks gamblin' drunk, fightin', laughin', cryin'
Mostly gamblin'. Playin' 'pups' wild deuces game
Doin' it, risking their twenty cents to try to win thirty
Price of bread, you know. You know, life ain't too bad here
No runnin' water, no fireplaces, huh, no houses even
Jus the kerosene tin and hessian bag humpies.
They say there's 'welfare' for blacks these days
But the mission looks the same to me. Seven I got
An' another one in the barrel—put there by the 'manager'
'Cause his wife cut him short or somethin'.
Nothin' changes. I don't ever see nothin' much
An' no-one asked me my view before.

1978

Mum

Fifteen dogs prowled
baying tense
unkempt and shaggy
hair and bones
marked out their form
and spoke of lean
and leaner times
at their old home
still faithful yet
as if to say
there's more than food
that makes us stay
a quality we feel and know
to make our very bristles glow

with love from those within
and passing through
the canvas door
I started in surprise
I saw
a woman lying on a bed
legs made of packing cases
dead — she never moved
the yellowed sheet
the tattered bedspread
at her feet
the squalor of the ragged tent
the greasy pots I near gave vent
to screams of outrage horror mind
raced crazily a pounding drum
a man's soft gentle voice 'My Mum
she's blind and seventeen
years of it I've never seen
the rhyme or reason for the act
they won't give us a house
the fact
speaks for itself the tent the bed
the dogs are better off' he said.
'My Mum she's blind she's now asleep
she'll wake up soon
the fact of it
she won't go nowhere
but the bed
Commission said no house
not fit
or Black or something and . . .'
he said
'the dogs live better in this land
and we'd do better dead
my Mum she's blind'
he said.

[1988]

Fay Zwicky

b 1933, Melbourne. Formerly a concert pianist. She taught English at the University of WA 1976–87, and is now a freelance writer. *Kaddish* (1982), *Ask Me* (1990).

Mrs Noah Speaks

[from *Ark Voices*]

Lord, the cleaning's nothing.
What's a pen or two?
Even if the tapir's urine
Takes the paint clean off
There's nothing easier.

But sir, the care!

I used to dream perpetually
About a boat I had to push
(yes, *push*) through a stony town
without water
There was no river and no sea and yet
I pushed a boat against a tide.
It wouldn't float although I pulled and
hauled, my flesh eddying,
drifting with the strain of it.
Is this a dream?
Fibre my blood, sir.

The speckled pigeon and the tawny owl
swoop by
             They coax me to the edge.

To save to save merely — no matter
what or whom — to save.

Sweep and push of waves against the sides.
Our raft is delicate and our fire
turns wood to ashes.

He takes it well
and Shem and Ham *do* help — you can't expect
too much of anyone can you and
Japhet's still a kid. Their wives are
young and tremble in the rain
their wits astray.

As soon as we're born
we're all astray — at least
You seem to think it's so or else
why this?

I know you promised us a landing but
what a price!
We're dashed from side to side
we strike through spray
the foam blinds Noah till he
cannot steer.
Even the mightiest creature cowers in his
stall panting, snorting in the welter,
bursting prayers upon your path
of righteousness.

Comfort enough I'm not.
To feed and clothe, to bind a scratch I can.

We once moved quiet in our lives
Looked steadily ahead. When I was small
there were no roads across the mountains
no boats or bridges over water.
We farmed, lived simple, circumscribed.
Our birds and beasts delivered their young
in peace.
            The trees grew tall and now and
then I pocketed a speckled egg, could climb
and peer into the nests of starlings.
Height and blossom.

Then we lived neighbourly with our birds.
Creation, your handiwork, was one.
No good and bad — just men and women.
But with your sages came the rub.
                              We tripped
over our charity. Duty-fettered, love
tumbled like a lightning-stricken tower.

Noah is incorruptible and good, a large
sweet soul.
Sir, I have tried to be!
But does the frog whose home was in a well
assail an ocean?
How does the summer gnat approach the ice?
The flood in which you throne us is to the
universe a puddle in a marsh.

                    Of all the myriad
creatures you have made, man is but one, the
merest tip of hair upon a stallion's rump.

Noah looks into space.
He sees the small as small
The great as great.
He sees, goes fearless at the sight.
I see the small as too little
the great as too much.
Does this diminish me?

He looks back to the past
grieves not over what is distant.
I mourn the wrack, the rock under the
blue sea, our old wound, the
dismantling storm and cannot
thank you.
                    Helpless with what I am
what can I do? This pitted flesh and
madness in my heart, rage at my fear
of you. Am I thus harmless?

Strangers in this ark, this one small 'Yes'
afloat on a vast 'No', your watery negative.

Noah stares impassive through the foam.
I trust in him although our woe, the
trap of my young body, cracked his trust
in me.
            I bend but do not break under your
chilling stars.

Even the wolves, the tigers must be fed
in these deep-laden waters. Else we are
all drowned bones.
                    Intercede with him
for me, speechless and unspoken to, the
comic keeper of his house.
My sons are fraught with wives, have
waded into deep waters.
A full ship and homeward bound — Yes,
I'm just about to lance the horse's leg.
A large sweet soul and incorruptible
I said. Or have I seen the great as
too much yet again?

> The speckled pigeon
> and the tawny owl have drawn me to the edge.
> The drowned folk call to me:
> Deliver us from harm!
>
> Deliver, sir, deliver them
> and all of us . . .

1982

Tiananmen Square

June 4, 1989

Karl Marx, take your time,
looming over Highgate on your plinth.
Snow's falling on your beard,
exiled, huge, hairy, genderless.
Terminally angry, piss-poor,
stuffed on utopias and cold,
cold as iron.

I'm thinking of your loving wife,
your desperate children and your grandchild
dead behind the barred enclosure of your brain.
Men's ideas the product, not the cause
of history, you said?

The snow has killed the lilacs.
Whose idea?
The air is frozen with theory.

What can the man be doing all day
in that cold place?
What can he be writing?
What can he be reading?
What big eyes you have, mama!
Next year, child, we will eat.

I'm thinking of my middle-class German grandmother
soft as a pigeon, who wept
when Chamberlain declared a war.
Why are you crying, grandma?
It's only the big bad wolf, my dear.
It's only a story.

There's no end to it.
The wolves have come again.
What shall I tell my grandchildren?

No end to the requiems, the burning trains,
the guns, the shouting in the streets, •
the outraged stars, the anguished face
of terror under ragged headbands
soaked in death's calligraphy.

Don't turn your back, I'll say.
Look hard.
Move into that frozen swarming screen.
How far can you run with a bullet in your brain?

And forgive, if you can, the safety of a poem
sharpened on a grieving night.

A story has to start somewhere.

1990

Jennifer Strauss

b 1933, Heywood, south-western Victoria. She has taught English at Monash University in Melbourne since 1964. *Winter Driving* (1981), *Labour Ward* (1988).

Loving Parents

Sometimes, night-waking, they made love
As if two strangers frantic to be known,
As if unfeaturing darkness stripped away
Affectionate disguises, long-term habits
Which daylight coupling decently assumed,
And laid the fierce nerves of loving bare.

Such times, they moved about their morning chores
Abstracted, in a sensual shadowed glow
Where suckling babies might bask mindlessly
But awkward older children, growing wise,
Looked askance, and bruised their egos' fists
Against that dark complicity which gave them being.

1975

Songs Our Mothers Teach Us

We teach our children early the analytic heart.
'Not mine,' we say
To the desolate weeping in the evening street
Which clicks some dozen of maternal ears
To clenched reception, though the hands still move

Stirring the sauce, setting the table, running the bath:
'Not mine.'
Switch off.

Our manly sons, schooled to the games of life,
As prompt as hurl a hand grenade can cast
A pronoun in the plural.
'Not ours,' they say
To the shattered town bleeding its fiery tears —
Setting the sights, pressing the trigger, dumping the bomb;
'Not ours.'
Switch on.

1975

Bluebeard Re-Scripted Version III: Sister Anne, Her Story

I'm writing it with my feet —
Small scuffs in sand the desert wind I know
Will easily erase; not lasting,
But it's mine. I ask you
How would *you* like to be listed
Among the *dramatis personae* merely
'Her sister' and have no lines
Except to answer the idiot question
'Is anyone coming? Do you see anyone coming?'
It's narrative isn't it? Of course they came.
Him first, rage-red, waving his sword
(Quite an erection) and then my family,
Father and brothers all in a band
Flogging their wretched horses through real heat.
Passion, revenge, a rescue? What a bore,
Predictable whichever way it ended —
I wouldn't know, I've walked off
The edge of the script, and sand
Has muffled the rumour of screaming and shouting.
Tonight I'll lie down with silence —
Better than Bluebeard, though I fancied him.
It was all I was taught to fancy,
The man of some other woman:
The mother's cherished son, the disconsolate widower,
The sister's husband with a roving eye.
I'm refusing my cues, am not convinced
My role's peripheral,
Desert and sand the only locations,
Myth the only mode. I'll walk, I'll sleep.
When I wake up, history will start.

1988

Tending the Graves

There are days when the dead will have nothing to do with us —
In summer mostly, when a dry wind from the north
Gusts up just as you enter the cemetery gates
And the roses are overblown, the gum trees stripping,
And you know the flowers you've brought will wither fast
And are besides the wrong size for the holder
And you've forgotten scissors, and something to carry water.

It's not reproach. They have no need to tell us 'You
Have given away my books, taken another lover into my bed,
Made of my children something I do not approve' — all that
We can say for ourselves. It is absolute absence.
They are so engrossed by death they refuse even to haunt us.
We must tend the grave and walk away; unrewarded,
Unreproached, unforgiven; our feet heavy with life.

1988

The Snapshot-Album
of the Innocent Tourist

This is a space for the President's
Rather splendid Palace,
Standing above
The not-so-picturesque
Riverflat shanties.
'Prohibido!' said the baby-faced boy
Whose gun was real,
'Prohibido!': I got the message
If not the shot.

This is a space for the corner
Where the student was beaten to death
And for the feet of workers
Stepping, they said, at morning
Round a pool of blood.
I couldn't focus it
For Christmas traffic
And besides it looked
Like any intersection, anywhere.

This space is for twenty working years
Erased from the centre
Of a teacher's life.
'It's good to be back,' he says
And smiles as if believing
The text can be restored:

All its pages,
The ungiven lectures, the burnt books,
The silenced words.

This is a space for the disbelief
Of the elegant woman
Whose perfume is charming
Like her apartment.
Only the tiniest hairline scar
Betrays the facial tuck, the will to deny:
'It was terrible,' she cries
'But nobody knew. Nobody spoke.
How could we know?'

This space is for the grandparents
Who hid a dangerous child,
Unregistered,
Infected by his father,
Who died 'resisting arrest', his mother
Who left for a meeting
And never came back,
Except in the set of his mouth
When the boy is angry, or laughs.

This is a space for all the disappeared
Who fade in other people's albums:
This is a space for courage
And for love,
For things that don't show up
In negatives.

1988

Vivian Smith

b 1933, Hobart. He taught French at the University of Tasmania, and since 1967 has taught English at the University of Sydney. *Selected Poems* (1985).

For My Daughter

Made from nothing: bud and rose,
kisses, water, mystery:
you who grew inside our need
run, in your discovery,

out of the garden's folded light,
out of the green, the fountain's spray,

past the shrubs, the dew-lit ferns,
out to the noise, the street, the day:

and stand, in your astonishment,
beneath the hanging heavy limes
(O my child, O my darling daughter,
summer was full of wars and crimes)

to see the foal, the clown, the doll,
the circus and procession band
march up the street and march away . . .
And so you turn and take my hand.

1967

The Man Fern near the Bus Stop

The man fern near the bus stop waves at me
one scaly feather swaying out of the dark,
slightly drunk with rain and freckled with old spores
it touches me with its slow question mark.

Something in the shadows catches at the throat,
smelling like old slippers, drying like a skin,
scraped like an emu or a gumboot stuck with fur,
straining all the time to take me in.

Cellophane crinkles in the fern's pineapple heart.
The fur parts slowly showing a crumpled horn.
A ruffled sea horse stands in swaying weed,
and held in cotton wool, a mouse unborn.

I look down at it now, a tiny toe, a crook,
remembering voices and growth without choice —
the buds of fingers breaking into power
and long fibres breaking in the voice.

1982

Night Life

Disturbed at 2 a.m. I hear a claw
scratching the window, tapping at the pane,
and then I realise, a broken branch,
and yet I can't turn back to sleep again.

Slowly, not to wake you, I get up,
thinking of food, perhaps a quiet read.
A cockroach runs across the kitchen floor,
its lacquered shell as quick and dry as seed.

Outside the chalice lily lifts its cup
in adoration to the mirrored moon,
full of purpose as it trembles there,
collecting drops of moisture on its spoon.

Noises of the night, it's all alive,
birds shifting in the steady trees,
slugs and snails eating fallen flowers,
a moth freighted with fragilities.

Nocturnal life, the other side of things,
proceeding whether we observe or not,
like rows and rows of brown coastal ants
transporting food from here to another spot.

[1988]

Margaret Scott

b 1934, UK; arrived in Australia 1959. She was a research assistant for the Education Department in Hobart, and since 1966 has taught English at the University of Tasmania. *Visited* (1983), *The Black Swans* (1988).

Grandchild

Early this morning, when workmen were switching on lights
in chilly kitchens, packing their lunch boxes
into their Gladstone bags, starting their utes in the cold
and driving down quiet streets under misty lamps,
my daughter bore a son. Nurses sponged him clean
as the glittering shingle of suburbs beside the river
waned to a scattered glimmer of pale cubes.
We met at half-past twelve in a ward crowded
with people busy with parcels and extra chairs.
A bunch of flowers fell on the floor. We passed
the baby round. His dark head lay in my hand
like a fruit. He seemed to be dwelling on something
half-remembered, puckering his brow, occasionally
flexing fingers thin and soft as snippets of mauve string.
Far below in the street lunch-time crowds flowed out
among the traffic. Girls went arm in arm on high
heels. An ambulance nosed into a ground-floor bay.
A clerk strode in the wind with a streaming tie.
Beyond the office blocks and the estuary, in Santa Fe,
Northampton or the other side of town, a young man
may be gripping a girl's hand as they climb upstairs.
She is wearing a cotton dress. Her sandals slip
on metal treads. She laughs, embarrassed, excited

at being desired so urgently in the
minutes before this grandchild's wife is conceived.
And his best friend, whose parents quarrel all day
about leaving Greece, is lying perhaps in his cot
on a balcony, watching his fat pink hands and woolly sleeves
swatting at puffs of cloud in the airy blue.
News he may break to our boy in some passage-way
in a house we've never seen is breeding now
in the minds of pensive children queuing by Red Cross
trucks, or curled like foetuses deep under warm quilts
as the long ship-wrecking roar of the distant sea
slides to the coming of night and fades away.

1988

from *Elegies*

M.F.C.S. 1928–1984

I

At ten to twelve by the grandfather clock
in the hall you stopped breathing in your sleep.
I put down the telephone and came back
to the study door — as I'd come for years
with questions, news and jokes —
meaning, I think, to tell you you were dead,
but the light of the lamp beat down
on the arm and seat of your chair
and the darkness filled with glimmering books
reeled and shook with your absence as though
from the long stroke of a black bell.
The cat was mewing, mewing down in the kitchen
and I went as on ordinary nights to open a door
but this was the first meeting with life
from the new world in which no search
could find you, so I watched wary of strangeness
as the pleased arch of its back wound round
my legs, and it strolled, taking breath for granted,
down the path. There was no wind.
Nothing but garden trees rising against
the glow of Saturday night and the pulse of silence.

II

Friends who mean to be kind speak of a happy release
and it's true that in the week before you died
you couldn't eat or walk, your mind was going.
You spoke of prisons and woke at night from
tormenting dreams of actions for negligence.

Between sips of Sustagen made at three in the
morning you called for documents, gave contrary
directions concerning capital trials and execution.
On the day of your death, your compassionate
philosopher's face broke in chaotic fragments —
a nose sharp as a fin, a flake of dark moustache,
ulcers, a tooth, a harsh bubbling snore.
But time like your bones collapsed in on itself.
Your waking eyes were blue. You said, 'Dear love,
dear love' as tenderly as on that summer night
in the dunes beyond the yacht club.
Holding your hand, I remembered how you sat
by my bed on the day our child was born and,
to take my mind off the pain, gave a most lucid elegant
disquisition on contingent and necessary statements.
The hearing's over now, the case is lost,
our past locked up beyond the reach of proof.

III

We kept ourselves to ourselves, had private jokes,
a language full of markers for buried stories.
We never called the police or saw a doctor.
Social workers left us well alone.
Only when you were dying the invaders came.
That body that knew mine by secret signs
was stripped, drugged, X-rayed and cut open.
Kind professionals asked about our income,
translating us into type on a set of forms.
No doubt in these after-days there's a bland jargon
for how by day and night I live without you
badgered by that idiot child who skulks
at the back of my mind, demanding, puzzled,
and fretful, where you've gone, expecting you back,
putting out too many plates, whining away
about a lack of justice. But only you
and I could catch the sub-text of what I'd say
if your ghost came round the corner, waving
your stick, smiling and glad to be home.
I always said you were too damned fair to live.

V

We go back to the sixties you and I,
to Kennedy shot in Dallas, everyone
quoting the figures on Vietnam, the Beatles
singing 'Strawberry Fields Forever' —

you always ready to tune to the loud world,
spending your passion on people we didn't know,
on far-off wars, remote injustices —
me in my mountain house, shut in by trees,
playing over and over again my worn records
of what we'd said or what we ought to have said
last time we'd met to part for the last time.
You moved fast, chain smoking, angry, divided,
addicted already to whisky and lost causes.
I was the great survivor, the single-minded,
hell-bent on making you happy at any price.
And so we lived together till you died.
Now in the eighties, refugees still crowd
in squalid camps, old wrongs, fresh massacres
still make the news, and I, having nothing left
but your charred bones, listen all day to my stack
of collector's items, all night to the wind
blowing down through the mountain trees.

1988

Antigone Kefala

b 1934, Braila, Romania, of Greek parents; moved to New Zealand in 1951 and to Australia in 1959, where she lives in Sydney. She has worked as a librarian and as an arts administrator. *European Notebook* (1988).

Barbecue

At our back
the forbidden house
and beyond
the convent on the hill
massive red.

The streets deserted
only we in the bald yard,
with the gum tree
fanning itself nervously,
eating raw meat laced
with black flies
drinking the parched wind
and making polite conversation
while the light poured on us
sizzling.

1978

The Place

I

The place was small, full of hills,
palm trees, almond trees, oleanders,
glass flowers falling from the sky
on the ascetic hills, the bare houses.
The ancients had been there looking for copper.

Around the courtyards in the dusk
grey men in army coats
followed the leader round the ramparts.
At night after the toll, the three
would come dressed up to count the souls.

We waited there two summers.
Tall birds with upturned beaks
picked us like grain.
We moved in herds
waited with patience to be fed
drank at the water places
between the walls our necks grew longer
stretching for the night.

II

The ships, we had heard, had sunk
weighed with the charity of the new world
that kept on feeding us with toys,
letters in foreign tongues
that we could not decipher.

We gave them to our silent children, onyx eyed,
brought up on wakes for spirits that had gone
and knew each drop that added the ingredients
to the day in the appointed measure.

For them, we looked at the cross roads
to find only the sound of running water
and the dusk settling in plum coloured
over the hills
the coolness of the evening full of promise.

III

They came in spring with the great winds
the buyers
walked through the gates in groups

their marrow discoloured
their eyes ashes
gestures full of charity.

Bidders, in markets for flesh
untouched by the taste of the coffee
and the scent of the water
on the hot stones.

IV
We travelled in old ships
with small decaying hearts
rode on the giant beast
uncertain
remembered other voyages
and the black depths
each day we feasted on the past
friends watching over
the furniture of generations
dolphins no longer followed us
we were in alien waters.

1978

David Malouf

b 1934, Brisbane, of a Lebanese father and an English mother. After a decade spent in
Europe, he taught English at the University of Sydney 1968–77. Also a novelist, he resides
alternately in Sydney and Tuscany. *Selected Poems* (1991).

Confessions of an Only Child

for my Sister

Two years five days between us, and my nose
(or rather, grandfather's)
put firmly out of joint. Then half the length
of a pool over the hundred metres dash
to my masculinity. You were like father, I like mother,
a happy compromise — though we were seldom on speaking terms
and scrapped like tigers mostly. I wrote you out
of my childhood, preferring
afternoons without you, a moony child practising thunder
by Czerny, Clementi,
to our closetings together through chicken pox, slow wet weeks
at the beach-house playing euchre for film-star swaps.

My afternoons in fact
were yours. The poems are also yours, and empty
without you. Now there are deaths
between us, and a marriage, three hectic stars
you've captured from the dark. They flare, they plunge away, go flying
down the wet beach. We are left
alone as in our earliest photograph: a stack of ruined sandcastles
between us, behind
the last patch of scrub, grey ring-barked trunks in winter sunlight; ahead
a night of carbide lamps. Like stars on brilliant claws battalions
of soldier crabs death-rattle
and wheel across the zodiac, sand granules
pour through my fist. The Pacific poised
on a day late in the 'Thirties rolls its thunder
towards us, pulled awry
by the moon. Our faces gather
their lines, their light, we grow like one another, the high cheekbones
of parents and other strangers
rise under the skin. We might be twins at last, with nothing
between us, no time at all. Burned to a blackness
we smile into the sun.

1974

Between Towns

On the north-west highway stranded, in open country near Dunedoo:
    a shadow by flashlight mends a wheel, the sky turns slowly
west over north. In frosty paddocks, lights, a fettler's camp
    or boys at early milking. It might be Sydney or Babylon
we left just after noon, and how far is it to the next
    town (I don't mean Coolah) that glows ahead, or the next star
we'll leap to over the ditch of dark? I share the time with hawk-moths
    that dance in the headlamps' flare or into the nightjar's maw, enormous
darkness between towns. At dawn the dormitory suburbs
    of Cerveteri rising ghostly through the weeds, dark horsemen gather
charge, and the bronze helm cleaves before a harder metal plunging
    deep into unknown empires, Knossos, Mycenae in the fields
below us, sinking with their weight of gold; at Chichen Itza
    worn granite climbs, and a whole city steps off into jungle
silence, thickening light — a legend barely kept alive,
    between towns, on the tongues of herdsmen in their cow-dance preserving
the classic consonants, a broken shard turned in the hand.

Between Towns: The ancient sites mentioned are, respectively, in central Italy (Cerveteri, in Etruria), Crete (Knossos), southern Greece (Mycenae) and Mexico (the Mayan city of Chichen Itza).

The darkness between towns is not deserted. Farmlights signal, or the sun
catches a roof or glances off a blade, something is held
    in trust. In the eyes of goatherds hunkered down beside a lake
in the steady, iron rain of Etruria, a city beckons,
    they rub their eyes and blink. The gold-tipped needle-towers of Florence
(or is it New York?) blaze out, they reach towards them, rush-hour traffic
    halts at the fording-place, the cook-fires of lost armies wink
from suburb to suburb now, dawn pickets shout, their white breath hanging
    still where a milkhorse clops along the narrow lane towards them,
a hunter tracking mammoth in the dark looks up astonished
    by the first rocket blasting into space where his spear-arm hurls it
far beyond brain or eye. Under the tongues of cattle, under
    the tails of comets now the dead look up from sea-shell middens
and stick-plough paddy-fields to the shuttle service between moons.

A town is a meeting-place: hands at the trestle table passing
down through a family a cup to be drunk from and kept safe
    a while out of children's reach; a group of neighbours setting forth
at dawn into unknown country, and where they stop to shoe a horse,
    or gnaw hard tack, is where their names shall ring for centuries.
The journey is into time. Grassheads sigh, deer lift their antlers
    alert, prepared to scatter, windows shine in stony paddocks
where strange humped cattle breathe. A town is what we are making for.
    Gaze round you. It might be here where two roads cross or somewhere over
the ridge where empty fields await our coming. No signposts name it
    yet or point directions. The next city we shall inhabit
is still in our saddlebags, in the dipper, flashing as we drink.
    If not this star, another — there where they shift in millions over
the grass. Already named they wait for us, and we are on
    our way, bearing the names their streets will bear. A moment only
in the darkness between towns, while shadows pause and change a wheel.

1974

An Ordinary Evening at Hamilton

The garden shifts indoors, the house lets fall
its lamp light, opens
windows in the earth

and the small stars of the grass, the night insects, needlepoint
a jungle more dense
than any tapestry, where Saturn burns, a snow owl's nest, and melons feed

their crystal with hot sugars of the moon. The Pacific
breaks at our table,
each grain

of salt a splinter of its light at midday, deserts
flare on the lizard's tongue. Familiar rooms
glow, rise through the dark — exotic islands; this house

a strange anatomy
of parts, so many neighbours in a thicket:
hair, eyetooth, thumb.

1974

Chris Wallace-Crabbe

b 1934, Melbourne. Also an influential critic, he has taught English at the University of Melbourne since 1968. *I'm Deadly Serious* (1988), *For Crying Out Loud* (1990).

Amphibious

Shall I say I remember, sort of,
the way a body remembers things,
two or three stick-in-the-mud steps
at an edge, then stooping in,
pushing off across that toffee-toned
slight swirling of leisurely water,
its barely discernible taste of earth
(which is part of being primaeval),
to and fro breaststroke, touching down
now onto softness, now on the smooth
bumpiness of water-fingered pebbles,
and once reaching up into
the lighter overlying medium
to pluck out of green shade a spray
of ever so gracefully descending
rivergum foliage?
                        Yes, I shall say it
with all the fervour of hands and feet
quite unaccustomed to abstraction,
feeling for those curved leaves now.

1985

That Radical Politics Is Impossible

You'll grow up,
you'll settle down,
they'll boil you down
into the common toffee,
knowing this:

someone has to scrape up
the fifty-one per cent
of requisite agreement;
somebody has to make
the whole caboodle work.

There will be no point in asking,
'What was my gift?
Where is my true note?'
We're happy as larry to pay you
not to find out.

Don't rock the boat
or you'll crack the bloody duco.
Don't bite the managers:
they were the boys who handed out
these oars and rowlocks

which you may choose to ignore.
So belt up
or put up or shut up because
to him which hath some gravy
shall gravy be given forever.

1985

Stuff Your Classical Heritage

Gull, grevillea, galvo, Gippsland, grit —
just singing out the chorus, bit by bit
will get me some purchase on the primal scene.

What do I say by seeing and then saying
a ragged strip of bark rips itself off
the slender limblike trunk of a manna gum

with faintest crumpling noise?
                              Call it said,
call it commitment to a twiggy particular
fawn-scumbled slope or terracotta roof.

By naming, I seem to crush the past
like a mattress, hard down in history's
rusty cabin-trunk: stick it in the cellar.

In a way, I preach the destruction of Europe,
that mental Europe which I love so much.
Cancel it. Smother it with ripe new words

or old ones triumphantly misapplied,
every solecism a seal of triumph
as light gilds a scraggy bacon-and-egg plant.

Keep Jehovah in his place with Bathurst burrs
where things are wiry, scrabbled, porous, drooped
for Oedipus romping through the undergrowth

every bit as gaudy as
those three dippingly quick rosellas
or a Violet Crumble wrapper.

1988

Hinge

As petite clouds
go fluttering prettily
over that highrise wedge of sky
Koori people
with plastic bags
crammed — perhaps — full of mystery

sit hunched or slummocking
on hot benches
at the knees of their health service.
One of them
slopes over to cadge
a cigarette if I have one,

but a dollar would do,
or history reversed.
There is geological spoor
under these black footpaths
and the past
keeps heading west.

While March sun
on these benches
burns a going century clean out
of our bones
the Second Coming
snoozes under chalk-blank newsprint.

Ah, dingy Gertrude Street,
the terrors of the earth are never quiet
and lost blue tribes
are dancing like the sound of crabs in a pot
on our thin coffin roof.

Forty cents will do
for a morning paper
from which to find
whether a bombing raid on Benghazi
proves much the same sort of thing
as it did in my boyhood.
                                    No.

                                                              1988

from *Sonnets to the Left*

II

    (i.m. Judah Waten)

As we grind into the worst decade for two
Or three or four, I swing around and see
Your bulky, suited, Russian form push through
This or that minor bookish jamboree
Smiling, and think of old hostility,
Those years when I watched you hard for Stalinism's
Cloven hoof and you (I'm sure) marked me
As bourgeois formalist. Time burns the isms.

Now Toorak and Balmain contrive to read
Marx as ur-text, perfect aesthetes delight
In cushioning off him too. The game is bent
Till we've become old colleagues with a need
For shoring words against the tide of night,
Praying the slow bitch History might relent.

                                                              1988

Thomas Shapcott

b 1935, Ipswich, south-eastern Queensland. He worked there as an accountant, and later, in Sydney, as an editor, arts administrator and novelist. A freelance writer, he lives in Melbourne. *Shabbytown Calendar* (1975), *Selected Poems* (rev. edn, 1989).

June Fugue

1.

Where shall we go? where shall we go?
— — We shall go to the Museum
What shall we see? is there lots to see?
— — We shall see rooms full of treasures
I want to see jewels and costumes
pharaohs and mummies
— — We shall spend hours among relics
  We shall be able to look hard
  at the blackened wrists of mummies.

2.

Do you remember that June day we drove into the mountains
we sang together all the songs from *Salad Days* and *My Fair Lady*?
— — Shall we sing those songs now? Remember them?
No I was thinking of the mountains   the walking track
through that patch of rainforest
— — And when we reached the sunlight
    I picked you an everlasting daisy.
You were always bringing me things.

3.

Do you remember the images the children said
'Why don't trees have two legs?'
'Daddy look at the broken moon'
'Mummy come in come inside you'll get the dark
    all over you.'
Children are so unalike.
They all draw bodies of sticks and daisies and circles.

4.

Where is that human hand? where is the Egyptian Mummy?
I'm sick of stuffed birds like the cat brought in.
— — It is a hand small as yours   but very dark
    dried out   a bundle of sticks
Where is it now show me   show me

5.

The attendants are bored   the children stop
and then laugh they move on   it is nothing
how shall I tell them the curse is true?
that out in the sunlight their shoulders are fingered
that already the things they bring in as Everlastings
have the smell of Museums   that once having drawn the circle
you will   get the dark all over you

1975

Near the School for Handicapped Children

His hat is rammed on
his shirt jerks at his body
his feet cannot hold in
     the sway   he cannot keep
                         still.
When I see his face it is freckled
to remind me of nephews
his limbs remind me of how straight
is my own spine and that I take my fingers
for granted.
He is waiting for the green light.
          My fingers clench
     I am hurt by my wholeness
     I cannot take my eyes from him
     I fear my daughter may be watching
He has been dressed carefully
     I'm here I'm here I'm here
his whole struggle rasps me like a whisper

and when the lights do change
     he skips across the road he
          skips he skips he dances and skips
               leaving us all behind like a skimming tamborine
               brittle with music.

1975

Town Edge

The last houses turn their backs
at the paspalum-seed paddocks
the last houses edge up together
and have watergreen lawns
with shrubs like a uniform's shirt-buttons.

The last houses are very lonely places
they have no grandparents or over-the-fence visitors
the automatic washtubs stain with babies' urine
squinting voices bite like sudden metal
whenever the children run in without wiping
the last houses wake in the night listening

there are no trees here no ghosts this is
the edge   tomorrow's world
somewhere a light gulps with surprise
somewhere a bed rocks rocks hard like the centre of being
unable to distinguish plunder or pain
somewhere there are voices laughing   calling cajoling

the new timber grunts the owners change already
already
they are not the last houses

1975

A Record of Flamenco Singing

How does a proud man sing
in our culture?
How does an old man sing
his own song here?
How do the sounds coil
out of the throat
how does the throat prepare
to take that offering?
We do not even spit phlegm
here, without embarrassment.

In my country
old men do not sing.
We have closed off
elegy, defiance.
We will not remember
the release possible
the terrible monkeys in the voice
taunting us
haunting
holding out ripe sweet grapes
bitter lemons
in handfuls, till we gulp.

1983

Judith Rodriguez

b 1936, Perth; educated in Brisbane. She has taught English at a number of colleges and universities, including La Trobe University in Melbourne 1969–85. She works as a publisher's consultant and teacher of writing, based in Melbourne. *New and Selected Poems* (1988).

About this woman:

green-eyed and could not give them to her children,
caresses her friends in thought, doubts they do likewise,
malingers and charms in fits and starts, dies daily.

About this woman:
wears no ring. Hangs on her husband, hang him,
to be the husband he could be, if he was;
if it takes fifty years. Faithfully mangles him
in words and thoughts, precarious vindications.

About this woman:
has heard of nymphs like wine; savagely inside
copes with turbid storm-water, and walls of sludge
it piled and can't shift now. The calm nymphs braid
light-runnels, a summer stilled. She dredges
in mixed minds at a quarry-mount of muddle:
where to dump, where gouge, whether
to abandon the site to flood,
worked faces flayed
with rubble in the flurry;

this woman.
Tuned to a tangible mode,
score half-composed, corrupt,
exultant, inharmonious, full of trouble . . .

1976

Water a Thousand Feet Deep

for Ensor

I stand washing up, the others have gone out walking.
Being at the best, I am homing in on the worst:

to choke in indifferent waves, over ears in ocean —
skim of earth's sweat — what immensities of salt fear
drench us and tighten — with children to save or lose,
the choice, as from old gods, which to consign to destruction:
how to riddle out waste and defiance? what line cast?

what crying hope hold to? for there is no deciding,
it acts itself, the damning sequence secret
as origin and universe, life as an improvisation
on terrors . . .

the tearaway undertow. But I never lose grasp on my son
or stop swilling plates and setting them to drain;

till blatantly the door. The boy ran ahead of the rest
and is home. I let him in panting, he trails me insisting
Hey, Mum, so close, there is so much floating known here
between us, have we trod the same waters? Hey, Mum,
is there water a thousand feet deep? Yes, I say,
emptying the sink, and give him figures, the soundings
of ocean trenches, which are after all within measure.
As if in the context of fathoms he'd made a mistake
and it mattered.

1976

Eskimo Occasion

I am in my Eskimo-hunting-song mood,
Aha!
The law is tundra   the car will not start
the sunlight is an avalanche   we are avalanche-struck at our breakfast
struck with sunlight through glass   me and my spoonfed daughters
out of this world in our kitchen.

I will sing the song of my daughter-hunting,
Oho!
The waves lay down   the ice grew strong
I sang the song   of dark water under ice
the song of winter fishing   the magic for seal rising
among the ancestor-masks.

I waited by water to dream new spirits,
Hoo!
The water spoke   the ice shouted
the sea opened   the sun made young shadows
they breathed my breathing   I took them from deep water
I brought them fur-warmed home.

I am dancing the years of the two great hunts,
Ya-hay!
It was I who waited   cold in the wind-break
I stamp like the bear   I call like the wind of the thaw

I leap like the sea spring-running.   My sunstruck daughters splutter
and chuckle and bang their spoons:

Mummy is singing at breakfast and dancing!
So big!

1976

A Concerned Aerial View

The moody thing a foot is.
Hands have to be clever,
cannot afford sulks,
'expressive' etc. of course —
effleurage and hypocrisy.
But your ground-down pitiful slab
unable, slung on bones,
awarded that immense callus, the heel,
for its earth-bound utility,
beaten up with work
and always at odds with the image —
how is a normal person
to get on with two lowgrade misfits
purple at the end of the bath
and come summer, dirty-shell-white
to your tanned shins?
And the huddle of degenerate toes!
Splay, play with them, they're never
less than conscious, never more
than first stumblers out of bed each day,
unwillingly from Eden. Poor things,
they consider the anemones.
At least as you confront them you think
they've got each other.
Even better, the nightly clambering
back into tree-memory:
I could be eloquent as leaves, they murmur,
feed my root . . .
All this time, the busybody hands
offer the overview, overkill
and totally convertible knowhow
to scoop kicks and the kickback:
I can do everything better
they say, let *me*, let *me* . . .

1982

In-flight Note

Kitten, writes the mousy boy in his neat
fawn casuals sitting beside me on the flight,
neatly, *I can't give up everything just like that.*
Everything, how much was it? and just like what?
Did she cool it or walk out? loosen her hand from his tight
white-knuckled hand, or not meet him, just as he thought
*You mean far too much to me. I can't forget
the four months we've known each other.* No, he won't eat,
finally he pays — pale, careful, distraught —
for a beer, turns over the pad on the page he wrote
and sleeps a bit. Or dreams of his Sydney cat.
The pad cost one dollar twenty. He wakes to write
It's naive to think we could be just good friends.
Pages and pages. And so the whole world ends.

1988

Les A. Murray

b 1938, Nabiac, NSW north-central coast; grew up on a dairy farm at nearby Bunyah, where he has resettled after residence in Canberra and Sydney. He has been a translator and a public servant, and a full-time poet since 1971. *The Boys Who Stole the Funeral* (1980), *The Vernacular Republic* (3rd edn, 1988), *Dog Fox Field* (1990).

The Breach

[from *The Police: Seven Voices*]

I am a policeman
it is easier to make me seem an oaf
than to handle the truth

I came from a coaldust town
when I was seventeen, because there was nothing
for a young fellow there

the Force drew me because of a sense I had
and have grown out of

I said to Ware once, Harry, you're the best
cop of the lot: you only arrest falls
he was amused

Ware: Special Sergeant Harry Ware (1897–1970), founder of the NSW Police Cliff Rescue Squad.

I seem to be making an inventory of my life
but in that house opposite, first floor
there is a breach
and me, in this body I am careful with,
I'm going to have to enter that house soon

and stop that breach

it is a bad one people could fall through
we know that three have
and he's got a child poised

I have struck men in back rooms late at night
with faces you could fall a thousand feet down
and I've seen things in bowls

the trick is not to be a breach yourself
and to stop your side from being one
I suppose

the sniper Spiteri, when I was just out of cadets —
some far-west cockies' boys straight off the sheep train
came up with their .303s and offered to help
they were sixteen years old

we chased them away, not doubting for a minute
they could do what they said
bury your silver the day we let that start

now I've said my ideals

Snowy cut, snow he cut . . .
A razor-gang hood my uncle claims he met
is running through my mind
in Woolloomooloo, wet streets, the nineteen twenties
dear kind Snowy Cutmore

Snowy cuts no more
he was a real breach

also, in our town, I
remember the old hand bowsers, that gentle apop-
poplexy of benzine in the big glass heads
twenty years since I saw them

There's a moment with every man who has started a stir

when he tires of it, wants to put it aside
and be back, unguilty, that morning, pouring the milk

that is the time to separate him from it
if I am very good I'll judge that time
just about right

the ideal is to keep the man and stop
the breach
that's the high standard

but the breach must close

if later goes all right
I am going to paint the roof of our house
on my day off.

1974

The Buladelah-Taree Holiday Song Cycle

1

The people are eating dinner in that country north of Legge's Lake;
behind flywire and venetians, in the dimmed cool, town people eat Lunch.
Plying knives and forks with a peek-in sound, with a tuck-in sound
they are thinking about relatives and inventory, they are talking about
    customers and visitors.
In the country of memorial iron, on the creek-facing hills there,
they are thinking about bean plants, and rings of tank water, of growing a
    pumpkin by Christmas;
rolling a cigarette, they say thoughtfully Yes, and their companion nods,
    considering.
Fresh sheets have been spread and tucked tight, childhood rooms have been
    seen to,
for this is the season when children return with their children
to the place of Bingham's Ghost, of the Old Timber Wharf, of the Big Flood
    That Time,
the country of the rationalized farms, of the day-and-night farms, and of the
    Pitt Street farms,
of the Shire Engineer and many other rumours, of the tractor crankcase furred
    with chaff,
the places of sitting down near ferns, the snake-fear places, the cattle-crossing-
    long-ago places.

2

It is the season of the Long Narrow City; it has crossed the Myall, it has
    entered the North Coast,
that big stunning snake; it is looped through the hills, burning all night there.
Hitching and flying on the downgrades, processionally balancing on the climbs,
it echoes in O'Sullivan's Gap, in the tight coats of the flooded-gum trees;
the tops of palms exclaim at it unmoved, there near Wootton.

Glowing all night behind the hills, with a north-shifting glare, burning behind
    the hills;
through Coolongolook, through Wang Wauk, across the Wallamba,
the booming tarred pipe of the holiday slows and spurts again; Nabiac chokes
    in glassy wind,
the forests on Kiwarrak dwindle in cheap light; Tuncurry and Forster swell
    like cooking oil.
The waiting is buffed, in timber villages off the higway, the waiting is buffeted:
the fumes of fun hanging above ferns; crime flashes in strange windscreens,
    in the time of the Holiday.
Parasites weave quickly through the long gut that paddocks shine into;
powerful makes surging and pouncing: the police, collecting Revenue.
The heavy gut winds over the Manning, filling northward, digesting the towns,
    feeding the towns;
they all become the narrow city, they join it;
girls walking close to murder discard, with excitement, their names.
Crossing Australia of the sports, the narrow city, bringing home the children.

3

It is good to come out after driving and walk on bare grass;
walking out, looking all around, relearning that country.
Looking out for snakes, and looking out for rabbits as well;
going into the shade of myrtles to try their cupped climate, swinging by one
    hand around them,
in that country of the Holiday . . .
stepping behind trees to the dam, as if you had a gun,
to that place of the Wood Duck,
to that place of the Wood Duck's Nest,
proving you can still do it; looking at the duck who hasn't seen you,
the mother duck who'd run Catch Me (broken wing) I'm Fatter (broken wing),
    having hissed to her children.

4

The birds saw us wandering along.
Rosellas swept up crying out *we think we think*; they settled farther along;
knapping seeds off the grass, under dead trees where their eggs were,
    walking around on their fingers,
flying on into the grass.
The heron lifted up his head and elbows; the magpie stepped aside a bit,
angling his chopsticks into pasture, turning things over in his head.
At the place of the Plough Handles, of the Apple Trees Bending Over, and of
    the Cattlecamp,
there the vealers are feeding; they are loosely at work, facing everywhere.
They are always out there, and the forest is always on the hills;
around the sun are turning the wedgetail eagle and her mate, that dour
    brushhook-faced family:

they settled on Deer's Hill away back when the sky was opened,
in the bull-oak trees way up there, the place of fur tufted in the grass, the
place of bone-turds.

5

The Fathers and the Great-Grandfathers, they are out in the paddocks all the
time, they live out there,
at the place of the Rail Fence, of the Furrows Under Grass, at the place of the
Slab Chimney.
We tell them that clearing is complete, an outdated attitude, all over;
we preach without a sacrifice, and are ignored; flowering bushes grow dull to
our eyes.
We begin to go up on the ridge, talking together, looking at the kino-coloured ants,
at the yard-wide sore of their nest, that kibbled peak, and the workers
heaving vast stalks up there,
the brisk compact workers; jointed soldiers pour out then, tense with acid;
several probe the mouth of a lost gin bottle:
Innuendo, we exclaim, *literal minds!* and go on up the ridge, announced by finches;
passing the place of the Dingo Trap, and that farm hand it caught, and the
place of the Cowbails,
we come to the road and watch heifers,
little unjoined devons, their teats hidden in fur, and the cousin with his loose-
slung stockwhip driving them.
We talk with him about rivers and the lakes; his polished horse is stepping
nervously,
printing neat omegas in the gravel, flexing its skin to shake off flies;
his big sidestepping horse that has kept its stones; it recedes gradually,
bearing him;
we murmur *stone-horse* and *devilry* to the grinners under grass.

6

Barbecue smoke is rising at Legge's Camp; it is steaming into the midday air,
all around the lake shore, at the Broadwater, it is going up among the
paperbark trees,
a heat-shimmer of sauces, rising from tripods and flat steel, at that place of
the Cone-shells,
at that place of the Seagrass, and the tiny segmented things swarming in it,
and of the Pelican.
Dogs are running around disjointedly; water escapes from their mouths,
confused emotions from their eyes; humans snarl at them Gwanout and
Hereboy, not varying their tone much;
the impoverished dog people, suddenly sitting down to nuzzle themselves;
toddlers side with them:
toddlers, running away purposefully at random, among cars, into big
drownie-water (come back, Cheryl-Ann!).
They rise up as charioteers, leaning back on the tow-bar; all their attributes
bulge at once;

swapping swash shoulder-wings for the white-sheeted shoes that bear them,
they are skidding over the flat glitter, stiff with grace, for once not travelling
    to arrive.
From the high dunes over there, the rough blue distance, at length they come
    back behind the boats,
and behind the boats' noise, cartwheeling, or sitting down, into the lake's
    warm chair;
they wade ashore and eat with the families, putting off that uprightness, that
    assertion,
eating with the families who love equipment, and the freedom from
    equipment,
with the fathers who love driving, and lighting a fire between stones.

7

Shapes of children were moving in the standing corn, in the child-labour
    districts;
coloured flashes of children, between the green and parching stalks,
    appearing and disappearing.
Some places, they are working, racking off each cob like a lever, tossing it on
    the heaps;
other places, they are children of child-age, there playing jungle:
in the tiger-striped shade, they are firing hoehandle machine guns, taking
    cover behind fat pumpkins;
in other cases, it is Sunday and they are lovers.
They rise and walk together in the sibilance, finding single rows irksome,
    hating speech now,
or, full of speech, they swap files and follow defiles, disappearing and
    appearing;
near the rain-grey barns, and the children building cattleyards beside them;
the standing corn, gnawed by pouched and rodent mice; generations are
    moving among it,
the parrot-hacked, medicine-tasseled corn, ascending all the creek flats, the
    wire-fenced alluvials,
going up in patches through the hills, towards the Steep Country.

8

Forests and State Forests, all down off the steeper country; mosquitoes are
    always living in there:
they float about like dust motes and sink down, at the places of the Stinging
    Tree,
and of the Staghorn Fern; the males feed on plant-stem fluid, absorbing that
    watery ichor;
the females meter the air, feeling for the warm-blooded smell, needing blood
    for their eggs.
They find the dingo in his sleeping-place, they find his underbelly and his
    anus;

they find the possum's face, they drift up the ponderous pleats of the fig tree,
    way up into its rigging,
the high camp of the fruit bats; they feed on the membranes and ears of bats;
    tired wings cuff air at them;
their eggs burning inside them, they alight on the muzzles of cattle,
the half-wild bush cattle, there at the place of the Sleeper Dump, at the place
    of the Tallowwoods.
The males move about among growth tips; ingesting solutions, they crouch
    intently;
the females sing, needing blood to breed their young; their singing is in the
    scrub country;
their tune comes to the name-bearing humans, who dance to it and irritably
    grin at it.

9

The warriors are cutting timber with brash chainsaws; they are trimming
    hardwood pit-props and loading them;
Is that an order? they hoot at the peremptory lorry driver, who laughs; he is
    also a warrior.
They are driving long-nosed tractors, slashing pasture in the dinnertime sun;
they are fitting tappets and valves, the warriors, or giving finish to a
    surfboard.
Addressed on the beach by a pale man, they watch waves break and are
    reserved, refusing pleasantry;
they joke only with fellow warriors, chaffing about try-ons and the police, not
    slighting women.
Making Timber a word of power, Con-rod a word of power, Sense a word of
    power, the Regs. a word of power,
they know belt-fed from spring-fed; they speak of being *stiff*, and being
    history;
the warriors who have killed, and the warriors who eschewed killing,
the solemn, the drily spoken, the life peerage of endurance; drinking water
    from a tap,
they watch boys who think hard work a test, and boys who think it is not a test.

10

Now the ibis are flying in, hovering down on the wetlands,
on those swampy paddocks around Darawank, curving down in ragged
    dozens,
on the riverside flats along the Wang Wauk, on the Boolambayte pasture flats,
and away towards the sea, on the sand moors, at the place of the Jabiru Crane.
leaning out of their wings, they step down; they take out their implement at
    once,
out of its straw wrapping, and start work; they dab grasshopper and ground-
    cricket
with nonexistence . . . spiking the ground and puncturing it . . . they swallow
    down the outcry of a frog;

they discover titbits kept for them under cowmanure lids, small slow things.
Pronging the earth, they make little socket noises, their thoughtfulness
     jolting down-and-up suddenly;
there at Bunyah, along Firefly Creek, and up through Germany,
the ibis are all at work again, thin-necked ageing men towards evening; they
     are solemnly all back
at Minimbah, and on the Manning, in the rye-and-clover irrigation fields;
city storemen and accounts clerks point them out to their wives,
remembering things about themselves, and about the ibis.

11

Abandoned fruit trees, moss-tufted, spotted with dim lichen paints; the fruit
     trees of the Grandmothers,
they stand along the creekbanks, in the old home paddocks, where the
     houses were;
they are reached through bramble-grown front gates, they creak at dawn
     behind burnt skillions,
at Belbora, at Bucca Wauka, away in at Burrell Creek,
at Telararee of the gold-sluices.
The trees are split and rotten-elbowed; they bear the old-fashioned summer
     fruits,
the annual bygones: china pear, quince, persimmon;
the fruit has the taste of former lives, of sawdust and parlour song, the tang
     of Manners;
children bite it, recklessly,
at what will become for them the place of the Slab Wall, and of the Coal Oil
     Lamp,
the place of moss-grit and swallows' nests, the place of the Crockery.

12

Now the sun is an applegreen blindness through the swells, a white blast on
     the sea-face, flaking and shoaling;
now it is burning off the mist; it is emptying the density of trees, it is
     spreading upriver,
hovering above the casuarina needles, there at Old Bar and Manning Point;
flooding the island farms, it abolishes the milkers' munching breath
as they walk towards the cowyards; it stings a bucket here, a teacup there.
Morning steps into the world by ever more southerly gates; shadows weaken
     their north skew
on Middle Brother, on Cape Hawke, on the dune scrub toward Seal Rocks;
steadily the heat is coming on, the butter-water time, the clothes-sticking
     time;
grass covers itself with straw; abandoned things are thronged with spirits;
everywhere wood is still with strain; birds hiding down the creek galleries,
     and in the cockspur canes;
the cicada is hanging up her sheets; she takes wing off her music-sheets.
Cars pass with a rational zoom, panning quickly towards Wingham,

through the thronged and glittering, the shale-topped ridges, and the
     cattlecamps,
towards Wingham for the cricket, the ball knocked hard in front of smoked-
     glass ranges, and for the drinking.
In the time of heat, the time of flies around the mouth, the time of the west
     verandah,
looking at that umbrage along the ranges, on the New England side;
clouds begin assembling vaguely, a hot soiled heaviness on the sky, away
     there towards Gloucester;
a swelling up of clouds, growing there above Mount George, and above
     Tipperary;
far away and hot with light; sometimes a storm takes root there, and fills the
     heavens rapidly;
darkening, boiling up and swaying on its stalks, pulling this way and that,
     blowing round by Krambach;
coming white on Bulby, it drenches down on the paddocks, and on the wire
     fences;
the paddocks are full of ghosts, and people in cornbag hoods approaching;
lights are lit in the house; the storm veers mightily on its stem, above the
     roof; the hills uphold it;
the stony hills guide its dissolution; gullies opening and crumbling down,
     wrenching tussocks and rolling them;
the storm carries a greenish-grey bag; perhaps it will find hail and send it
     down, starring cars, flattening tomatoes,
in the time of the Washaways, of the dead trunks braiding water, and of the
     Hailstone Yarns.

13

The stars of the holiday step out all over the sky.
People look up at them, out of their caravan doors and their campsites;
people look up from the farms, before going back; they gaze at their year's
     worth of stars.
The Cross hangs head-downward, out there over Markwell;
it turns upon the Still Place, the pivot of the Seasons, with one shoulder
     rising:
'Now I'm beginning to rise, with my Pointers and my Load . . .'
hanging eastwards, it shines on the sawmills and the lakes, on the glasses of
     the Old People.
Looking at the Cross, the galaxy is over our left shoulder, slung up highest in
     the east;
there the Dog is following the Hunter; the Dog Star pulsing there above
     Forster; it shines down on the Bikies,
and on the boat-hire sheds, there at the place of the Oyster; the place of the
     Shark's Eggs and her Hide;
the Pleiades are pinned up high on the darkness, away back above the
     Manning;

they are shining on the Two Blackbutt Trees, on the rotted river wharves, and
    on the towns;
standing there, above the water and the lucerne flats, at the place of the
    Families;
their light sprinkles down on Taree of the Lebanese shops, it mingles with
    the streetlights and their glare.
People recover the starlight, hitching north,
travelling north beyond the seasons, into that country of the Communes, and
    of the Banana:
the Flying Horse, the Rescued Girl, and the Bull, burning steadily above that
    country.
Now the New Moon is low down in the west, that remote direction of the
    Cattlemen,
and of the Saleyards, the place of steep clouds, and of the Rodeo;
the New Moon who has poured out her rain, the moon of the Planting-times.
People go outside and look at the stars, and at the melon-rind moon,
the Scorpion going down into the mountains, over there towards Waukivory,
    sinking into the tree-line,
in the time of the Rockmelons, and of the Holiday . . .
the Cross is rising on his elbow, above the glow of the horizon;
carrying a small star in his pocket, he reclines there brilliantly,
above the Alum Mountain, and the lakes threaded on the Myall River, and
    above the Holiday.

1977

The Future

There is nothing about it. Much science fiction is set there
but is not about it. Prophecy is not about it.
It sways no yarrow stalks. And crystal is a mirror.
Even the man we nailed on a tree for a lookout
said little about it; he told us evil would come.
We see, by convention, a small living distance into it
but even that's a projection. And all our projections
fail to curve where it curves.
                    It is the black hole
out of which no radiation escapes to us.
The commonplace and magnificent roads of our lives
go on some way through cityscape and landscape
or steeply sloping, or scree, into that sheer fall
where everything will be that we have ever sent there,
compacted, spinning — except perhaps us, to see it.
It is said we see the start.
                    But, from here, there's a blindness.
The side-heaped chasm that will swallow all our present
blinds us to the normal sun that may be imagined

shining calmly away on the far side of it, for others
in their ordinary day. A day to which all our portraits,
ideals, revolutions, denim and deshabille
are quaintly heartrending. To see those people is impossible,
to greet them, mawkish. Nonetheless, I begin:
'When I was alive — '
                              and I am turned around
to find myself looking at a cheerful picnic party,
the women decently legless, in muslin and gloves,
the men in beards and weskits, with the long
cheroots and duck trousers of the better sort,
relaxing on a stone verandah. Ceylon, or Sydney.
And as I look, I know they are utterly gone,
each one on his day, with pillow, small bottles, mist,
with all the futures they dreamed or dealt in, going
down to that engulfment everything approaches;
with the man on the tree, they have vanished into the Future.

1977

The Tin Wash Dish

Lank poverty, dank poverty,
its pants wear through at fork and knee.
It warms its hands over burning shames,
refers to its fate as Them and He
and delights in things by their hard names:
rag and toejam, feed and paw —
don't guts that down, there ain't no more!
Dank poverty, rank poverty,
it hums with a grim fidelity
like wood-rot with a hint of orifice,
wet newspaper jammed in the gaps of artifice,
and disgusts us into fierce loyalty.
It's never the fault of those you love:
poverty comes down from above.
Let it dance chairs and smash the door,
it arises from all that went before
and every outsider's the enemy —
Jesus Christ turned this over with his stick
and knights and philosophers turned it back.
Rank poverty, lank poverty,
chafe in its crotch and sores in its hair,
still a window's clean if it's made of air
and not webbed silver like a sleeve.
Watch out if this does well at school
and has to leave and longs to leave:
someone, sometime, will have to pay.

Lank poverty, dank poverty,
the cornbag quilt breeds such loyalty.
Shave with toilet soap, run to flesh,
astound the nation, run the army,
still you wait for the day you'll be sent back
where books or toys on the floor are rubbish
and no one's allowed to come and play
because home calls itself a shack
and hot water crinkles in the tin wash dish.

1990

J. S. Harry

b 1939, Adelaide, and educated there. She lives in Sydney. *The Deer under the Skin* (1971),
A Dandelion for Van Gogh (1985).

a shot of war

while those disintegrated by exocet
are unable to be present,
mrs thatcher — well wrapped
against the 'killing' chill
by a several foot
thickness of photographers
& 'fortified'
by the champagne-bubble-knowledge
that the war
was 'justified' — politically —
by being a success — in general —
with the british public —
& — in particular —
had improved
her popularity,
in january 1983
visits the falkland islands,
lays wreaths   on the ground
          above
'the british war-loss' —
& 'plays'
at being the one
to 'fire'
a military gun

a salon hair-do's blown to pieces
by the force of the falkland gales
which, earlier, pushed up those seas
through which, on which, & under which

particular, british, & argentinian,
soldiers, sailors, & de-planed airmen
were struggling, freezing, & dying,
& she 'jumps' like an ordinary
first-time-soldier
pushed back   by the noise
& power of the gun

'kittenish'
behaviour drops from her
at this sound   so 'like'
a shot of war

underground the
recovered, drowned, burned, shot,
blown up, or frozen
are unable to oblige
by 'doing it again'
for the publicity picture

1985

wind painting

lake birds in wind
ride a bucking
saddle of water

afghan dogs
float in the wind
their tresses laid back
like the hair of the willow

they are dancing under

the wind's water

like a film of themselves-
in-slow-motion

the wind buckets
the lake's surface

slops tilt
over the brim

the coots
ride it out on the slant
sliding & riding
in the sunblack light

which pinks the skin
of the pelican's
beak membrane round
the lump
of the frog he is swallowing
— there — in the lee by the willow —
hawk makes the high hill
over the tossing pine trees
spire of his hunting site
& the redbrowed finches & little birds
evanesce in the short grass
blown on screams of panic
thin as grass seeds

entering the invisible

there is one fat gold
dandelion for van gogh
tethered by its own sap
in the black damp shade
by the clump of horseshit

1985

Geoff Page

b 1940, near Grafton, north-eastern NSW, on a pastoral property. He teaches in a secondary school in Canberra. *Selected Poems* (1991).

Grit

A doxology

I praise the country women
of my mother's generation
who bred, brought up and boasted
six Australians each —
the nearest doctor fifty miles
on a road cut off by flood;
the women who by wordless men
were courted away from typewriters
and taught themselves to drive —
I praise their style
in the gravel corners.
I praise the snakes they broke in two
and the switch of wire they kept in a cupboard.
I praise what they keep and what they lose —

the long road in to the abattoirs,
the stare which cures
a stockman of shooting swans.
I praise the prints, the wide straw brims
they wore out to the clothes line;
I praise each oily crow that watched them.
I praise the tilting weather —
the dry creeks and the steady floods
and the few good weeks between.
I praise each column in the ledger
they kept up late by mosquito and lamp-light;
the temerity of the banker
reining them in at last — or trying;
the machinations for chequered paddocks
swung on the children's names;
the companies just one step ahead;
the tax clerk, in his way, also.
I praise each one of their six children
discovering in turn
the river in its tempers
the rapids and the river trees;
the children who grew up to horse sweat
and those who made it to the city.
I praise the stringy maxims
that served instead of prayers;
also the day that each child found
a slogan not enough,
surprising themselves in a camera flash
and bringing no extra paddocks.
I praise the boast of country women:
they could have been a wife
to any of a dozen men
and damn well made it work.
I praise what I have seen
to be much more than this.
I praise their politics of leather;
the ideologies in a line of cattle;
the minds that would not
stoop to whisky.
I praise their scorn
for the city of options, the scholars
in their turning chairs and air-conditioned theories.
I praise also that moment
when they headed off in tears —
the car in a toolshed failing to start,
a bootfull of fencing wire.

I praise the forty years
when they did not. I praise
each day and evening of their lives —
that hard abundance year by year
mapped in a single word.

1980

Clarence Lyric

for Alec and Penelope Hope

Surrounded by his
Pills and bottles
The old man's heaped
In bed at last
Washed in sidelong
From the world
Which circles seaward
With his past

Carpet snakes
With rats and swallows
Weave their close
Dependent lives
Silverfish
Invade the paintings
Whiteants hollow
Out the piles

A grandson and his
Wife move in
Rational with
Paint and saw
Three children spread
Into the rooms
Banging through the
Cedar doors

One soon lost
To outer paddocks
Another buoyant
On her smile
A third obscurely
Stalled by fiction
In a chair not
Quite in style

Snakes slide from
The long verandah
Rats go back
To tractor sheds
All morning through
The polished glass
A man stares outwards
From the dead

Sees the river
Skimmed with wind
Hears the children
Start to fight
The afternoon
Goes on forever
The westward pools
Are filled with light

1988

Geoffrey Lehmann

b 1940, Sydney. He has worked as a solicitor and lectures in taxation law at the University of Sydney. *Ross' Poems* (1978), *Children's Games* (1990).

from *Ross' Poems*

20

A vertical line through our roof
would intersect
with stars somewhere in space.
(There are other Spring Forests in the sky
and children crying. The stars
are a million mirrors of the earth.)
Closer to home this line
might bisect the moon's molten core,
and pass through
radiation belts,
the ozone filtering out the ultraviolet,
a tawny frogmouth flying
with a moth in its beak,
frost on our galvanized roof,
a kerosene pressure lamp perched on a book,
various texts on animal husbandry,

Ross' Poems: a book-length poem in 74 sections, in which the central character reflects on his life on the farm which he established and named 'Spring Forest'. The poem is based on real people.

some short stories
and a cherrywood pipe
I have lost for years and not yet found
(that's wishful thinking —
I probably lost it in some paddock
where my eyes will never gaze down)
down through pine floorboards,
a ginger and black guinea-pig asleep
beneath the house
and into red Koorawatha earth,
earth with only one need —
water for the green life chains.

If I tired of vertical lines
I could draw a horizontal line
through this fire of ironbark logs
(with its two sounds —
the billowing and beating
of rushing blue-red air,
and the dry cindering and splitting
of timber)
a line extending through the curl
of steam from the iron kettle
warming on the flagstones,
through my moleskin trousers
as I sit on an old car seat from the Morris
(my favourite low-level armchair)
just missing Olive's legs
busily gathering tea-things,
on through the bedroom with its black piano
carved with flowers and mandolins
(how the steel strings and sounding-board
wince in our draconian ranges of temperature —
the felt hammers decayed
when my wife the musician
married me and a farm)
through the weatherboards
and a stand of red geraniums,
on past the trunk of a giant dead wattle
(I don't remove old friends,
as birds like to perch in bare branches)
and through the chicken-wire enclosure
I keep around the house and garden,
past some dogs and a fruiting fig-tree,
past the cough of a fox.
I jump up with a gun and that's where that line ends.
But it's no use. Try shooting ghosts.
I come back inside.

Drinking a cup of cocoa
I draw a circle around the house
starting with the metal windmill
and creek where the ducks paddle,
but that's too wide,
I'll start my circle in closer
among some grass. It collects a hen
in a crater of dust, continues
through the bee-boxes with their new white paint,
on past my antique steamroller
'the slumbering giant'
and then I fetch up against that fox again
(or is it my mind?)

We have cosmic rays and cow manure,
flowers and a rusting dry-cleaners' van,
but there's no line around here
that will intersect a decent toilet or bathroom.

Through the dimensions I do not understand
I move
a column of living water.

                                                          1976

Parenthood

I have held what I hoped would become the best minds of a generation
Over the gutter outside an Italian coffee shop watching the small
Warm urine splatter on the asphalt — impatient to rejoin
An almond torta and a cappuccino at a formica table.
I have been a single parent with three children at a Chinese restaurant
The eldest five years old and each in turn demanding
My company as they fussed about in toilets while my pork sate went cold.
They rarely went all at once; each child required an individual
Moment of inspiration — and when their toilet pilgrimage was ended
I have tried to eat the remnants of my meal as they all twisted
Beneath the table, screaming and grabbing in a scrimmage.
I have been wiping clean the fold between young buttocks as a pizza
I hoped to finish was removed from a red and white checked table cloth.
I have been pouring wine for women I was anxious to impress
When a daughter ran for help through guests urgently holding out
Her gift, a potty, which I took with the same courtesy
As she gave it, grateful to dispose of its contents so simply
In a flurry of water released by the pushing of a button.
I have been butted by heads which told me to go away and I have done so,
My mouth has been wrenched by small hands wanting to reach down to
    my tonsils

As I lay in bed on Sunday mornings and the sun shone through the slats
Of dusty blinds. I have helpfully carried dilly-dalliers up steps
Who indignantly ran straight down and walked up by themselves.
My arms have become exhausted, bouncing young animals until they fell
    asleep
In my lap listening to Buxtehude. 'Too cold,' I have been told,
As I handed a piece of fruit from the refrigerator, and for weeks had to warm
Refrigerated apples in the microwave so milk teeth cutting green
Carbohydrate did not chill. I have pleasurably smacked small bottoms
Which have climbed up and arched themselves on my lap wanting the report
And tingle of my palm. I have known large round heads that bumped
And rubbed themselves against my forehead, and affectionate noses
That loved to displace inconvenient snot from themselves onto me.
The demands of their bodies have taken me to unfamiliar geographies.
I have explored the white tiles and stainless steel benches of restaurant
    kitchens
And guided short legs across rinsed floors smelling of detergent
Past men in white with heads lowered and cleavers dissecting and
    assembling
Mounds of sparkling pink flesh — and located the remote dark shrine
Of a toilet behind boxes of coarse green vegetables and long white radishes.
I have badgered half-asleep children along backstreets at night, carrying
Whom I could, to my van. I have stumbled with them sleeping in my arms
Up concrete steps on winter nights after eating in Greek restaurants,
Counting each body, then slamming the door of my van and taking
My own body, the last of my tasks, to a cold bed free of arguments.
I have lived in the extreme latitudes of child rearing, the blizzard
Of the temper tantrum and my own not always honourable or wise response,
The midnight sun of the child calling for attention late at night,
And have longed for the white courtyards and mediterranean calm of
    middle age.
Now these small bodies are becoming civilized people claiming they are not
Ashamed of a parent's untidy garden and unpainted ceilings which a
    new arrival
With the forthrightness of the infant complains are 'old'.
And the father of this tribe sleeps in a bed which is warm with arguments.
Their bones elongate and put on weight and they draw away into space.
Their faces lengthen with responsibility and their own concerns.
I could clutch as they recede and fret for the push of miniature persons.
And claim them as children of my flesh — but my own body is where I
    must live.

1990

Kate Llewellyn

b 1940, Tumby Bay on Eyre Peninsula, SA. She worked in Adelaide as a nurse and a gallery owner. Now a full-time writer, she lives at Leura, in the Blue Mountains, NSW. *Luxury* (1985), *Honey* (1988).

Theatre

With my legs in stirrups
I pushed you out —
it was like a race
with life the prize
(and as tricky as knitting under water)

I felt glad but that's all

they wheeled in the Father
and the Doctor said his reward
was in such scenes

a starfish of embarrassment
shrank
beached
I was a prop in their play

I wept all night
because no one had mentioned
responsibility
my face began to fall
in frightened pieces
on the floor

at my parents' home
ten dressing-gowned days later
a whiskey bottle beside the bed
and a baby
and a dummy
and me the Mummy

after your bath
my Father took out the scales
and like a lump of butter
half ounce anxious
my Mother weighed you

the petals of your soles
fluttered on the edge

now with a top hat
and swinging hair
you're on the stage
and wowing them
and they clap
and slowly I begin to clap
a stranger

1982

Yellow Stockings

She was five
in skinny yellow stockings
holding Father's hand
in the street

every second moment
happiness raised her heel
stuttered her toe
and stretched her
up to his face

I suppose
she'll go on
reliving
fragments
of this acceptance
from Daddy
with a dozen men
who
no matter
how she teaches it
aren't him

1982

Breasts

As I lean over to write
one breast warm as a breast from the sun
hangs over as if to read what I'm writing
these breasts always want to know everything
sometimes exploring the inside curve of my elbow
sometimes measuring a man's hand
lying still as a pond
until he cannot feel he is holding anything
but water
then he dreams he is floating

in the morning my breast is refreshed
and wants to know something new
although it is soft it is also ambitious
we never speak
but I know my breast knows me more than I do
prying hanging over fences
observant as a neighbour
or eager as a woman wanting to gossip
they tell me nothing
but they say quite a lot about me

there is a dark blue river vein here
straggling down taking its time
to the little pale strawberry
picked too soon and left too long
in the punnet in a warm shop

when I lie
these breasts spread like spilt milk
and standing naked in the sea
float like figs
as you will realise
these are my body's curious fruit
wanting to know everything
always getting there first
strange as white beetroot
exotic as unicorns
useless as an out of order dishwasher
more of a nuisance than anything else

some men seem to think highly of them
peering and staring
what they don't know is the breast stares straight back
interested as a reporter

some love them
and invest them with glamour
but like life they are not glamorous
merely dangerous

1985

Helen (1)

Was she pushed
or did she jump
into his boat
watching while they loaded
in the furniture

it must have been a rough trip
Helen and the furniture
lying about
among the stench of oarsmen
she was probably ill for days

and what did that so-called trollop
Helen think
when she heard they were coming
for revenge

after all she knew I guess
they could hardly shout
as they brandished their swords
'And what about that footstool?
I was very fond of that
give it back'
or 'Those lovely gilded bed ends
return them or I'll kill you now
and leave you for the air'

and sheltering behind her hair
did she think 'What a fuss
all over me they say
they had to dress it up
and call it me
a raid's a raid
but it was just too impertinent
to clear the palace out
any one would be very wild
to have to stand at home
so I suppose I'll just have to bear
the blame
I realise of course
they could hardly say
the furniture that launched
a thousand ships'

1985

Jan Owen

b 1940, Adelaide, and lives there. She has worked as a librarian, and in recent years as a teacher of writing. *Boy with a Telescope* (1986), *Fingerprints on Light* (1990).

Mirror Image

for Balázs

'Twenty-nine years ago; and only yesterday,'
says Balázs, slapping at a fly.
We sit beside a bottle underneath his vines
and watch the football arc between his sons.

'Check through the corner one,' the sergeant says,
'and make it short and sweet. Take a couple of men.'
(Seventeen-year-olds still nervous with a gun.)
It's an office block like most
down the derelict street;
he keeps a good five metres ahead,
tries the rooms along each corridor
and beckons the two boys on.
They reach the third floor
breathing easier now.
The Council Chamber's here,
empty but for a tangle of chairs
at the northern window end
(unseemly three-day corpses,
wooden legs in the air);
dried into the floor — blood-stains,
and, seeping through the shattered panes,
the distant dialogue of cross-fire;
directly opposite him — another door.
He notes the fact an instant before
it opens sharply and his counterpart —
the hated AVO uniform of green —
levels his gun and time is not.
They freeze. Somewhere beyond,
the seconds slide away;
between their eyes the slender lifeline holds
across the mirror of air.
'*Döntetlen baratom azt hiszem*':
Stalemate I think, my friend.

AVO: the security police.

Each slightly lowers his gun
and slowly, eyes still locked, takes one step back.
The two doors close together, softly as hands on a prayer.
'*Senki sincs ott,*' each says to his men:
Nobody there.

'In Hungary we used to say
"*Neha a masodik alkalom jön elöször*" —
sometimes the second chance comes first.'
He's silent, years away.
The day is insubstantial, seems to float
in the dry gum-scented heat.
Only the football's thud,
steady as the beat of some huge heart,
holds us in time and space.
He rouses himself to swear:
'*Az anyad*, off the kohlrabi, *rossz gyerekek,*'
then pours us another beer.
The head on each glass whispers small talk;
we blow the froth into the air.

1986

Young Woman Gathering Lemons

The apronful sits on the swell of her belly,
that taut new world she merely borders now.
Above, a hundred pale suns glow;
she reaches for one more and snags her hair.
Citron, amber, white, a touch of lime;
the rind of colour cools her palm.
Extra tubes and brushes she would need —
a three in sable, or a two
should catch the gleam around each pore.
Such yellow! If there were only time.
She presses to her face
its fine sharp scent of loss
then sinks her forehead onto her wrist
— the tears drip off her chin —
till the child tugs at her dress.
She kneels to hug him close and breathe him in:
'Who's got a silly old mother, then?'
It dizzies her, the fragrance of his skin.
He nuzzles under the hair come loose.
The fallen lemons, nippled gold,
wait round them in the grass.

1986

Metro

Buskers, somewhere at Châtelet —
their plainsong sounding the corridors for sky
raised transept, nave, and vault,
flooding them with unearthly light,
a silvery puzzlement the soul must feel
roaming artery, neurone, bowel.
At Tuileries a small drunk man lurched on,
slumped down and breathed in my hair. The train's
precipitate birth hurled us along
a darkness beyond the reach of song.
'Un homme seul, tu comprends.' I looked away
hoping he wouldn't vomit or cry.
'Tu comprends pas la solitude?'
He kept it up well past Concorde:
'English? I understand English. Look,'
he searched his coat for a paperback —
it was Gulliver clawing out at us
from the grip of a leering giantess.
He followed a black girl at L'Étoile
but missed the exit. I went up in the spill
of feet to a rush of wintry air
and the Champs Élysées plane trees sifting stars.
You could take wrong turns and trains for hours
down there—the labyrinth breeds on emptiness,
claims any outcast. Sometimes the choice is just
two different ways of being lost,
soul and seul are both importunate.
But I wish I'd smiled; these words come too late.

1990

Andrew Taylor

b 1940, Warrnambool, south-western Victoria. He has taught English at the University of Adelaide since 1971. *Selected Poems* (rev. edn, 1988), *Folds in the Map* (1991).

A Nocturne in the Corner Phonebox

Someone is playing a trombone
in the telephone box outside my room.
It's 1 a.m.,
and he's removed the globe.
He's playing a melancholy cadenza
probably over the S.T.D.
to his girl in Sydney.

I can imagine . . .
she's curled to the telephone
listening to that impossible music
a smile curving her face.
I wonder if he has enough change
for all those extensions.
Could he reverse the charge?

Somebody called Hugh Adamson
blares out a nocturne in a phonebox.
His father's old and dying,
his mother's dead, his girl's away,
he's very sad, his nocturne's very sad,
his trombone blares and flares and says
'He's very sad, yair yair, he's very sad'.

Maybe he's only playing to a friend
in East St Kilda.
Maybe he hasn't any change.
Someone is playing a trombone — impossible —
in the phonebox with the door shut.
I've no idea who he is. I'm waiting
for my phone to ring. I like this music.

1971

An Unbelievably Tidy Profusion

The land drops here faithlessly
to a sandy melaleuca swamp
then to the sea. From the house
we can see its ruled horizon through a gap
in the camphor laurels. Now and then
a ship passes. One night
the pawpaw near where I'm sitting
was torn by fruit bats. They descended
with a clatter of leather wings
like a delegation of briefcases
where I couldn't see them. The snarls
and snorting the other side of the house
mean koalas, though those restless
footsteps on the board floors
are the children's. Each night
they wander into my dreams as they grope
to the toilet. The sea shines
in the morning, while usually
the mountains north are hidden by cloud
till 10 a.m. We haven't seen

snakes yet, except one
an eagle was feeding on near the gate
this afternoon. We avoid
long grass. Yesterday
two great goannas on the road
debated noiselessly, heads high
and immobile. For three days
earwigs in every cranny —
cane seats, under leaves, even
in the ceiling joists.
And then as suddenly they were gone.
The mountains disappear too
and the sea. The children disappear
into their thoughts, and for whole mornings
hardly come back. There are large
and exotic insects with hard shells
and butterflies like scraps of satin
floating in the heat. Today
I emptied a bag of sodden salt
on a tray in the sun and watched it steam.
The night we arrived it rained — well
rivers poured from the sky, we shod
our heads and ran barefoot. Next morning
the sun broiled us. Lychees
and avocados and behind the house
a gully hides its shrilling secret
of rain forest — palms, vines, messmate,
fern, an unbelievably tidy
profusion. When we first arrived
I tossed a small bug from the door
and a lizard half as thick as my finger
snapped it from the air. The sea
polishes its thin horizon
over the melaleucas and pines
below us. After lunch
the kids are elsewhere. We make love
in the emptiest of rooms
in this empty house. Its polished boards
shine with a kind of sweat. Far off
a tractor mutters against a slope.
Windows glaze with the sun's glare.
This empty and grey airiness expands
as we touch, contracts
and expands until our heat
floods us with sweat. At the gate
camphor laurels and figs. Spiders

straddle webs two metres across
that flap like sails. At evening
the sea disappears and a close dark
fills with the sounds of feeding
and being fed on. Footsteps
through the night. This house —
so empty of furniture,
furnished so well.

1986

Roger McDonald

b 1941, Young, southern NSW. He was an influential poetry editor in Brisbane in the
1970s. He farms at Braidwood, south-eastern NSW, and is also a novelist. *Airship* (1975).

Two Summers in Moravia

That soldier with a machinegun bolted
to his motorcycle, I was going to say
ambled down to the pond to take
what geese he wanted; but he didn't.

This was whole days before the horizon trembled.

In the farmyard all the soldier did
was ask for eggs and milk.
He and the daughter (mother sweeping)
stood silent, the sky rounded
like a blue dish.

This was a day
when little happened,
though inch by inch everything changed.
A load of hay narrowly crossed the bridge,
the boy caught a fish underneath in shade,
and ducks quarrelled in the reeds.
Surrounded by wheat, everyone heard the wind
whisper, at evening, as though grain already threshed
was poured from hand to hand.

This was a day possible to locate, years later,
on a similar occasion; geese alive,
the sky uncracked like a new dish,
even the wheat hissing with rumour.

1975

1915

Up they go, yawning,
the crack of knuckles dropped
to smooth the heaving
in their legs, while some,
ashamed, split bile
between their teeth,
and hum to drown their stomachs.

Others touch their lips
on splintered wood
to reach for home —
'a bloke's a mug'
thinks one (who sees
a ringbarked hill)
another hisses drily
(leaping burrs).

All dreaming,
when the whistle
splits the pea, as up
they scramble, pockets fat
with Champion Flake
in battered tins,
and letters wadded thick
from Mum (who says
'always keep
some warm clothes on . . .')

Up from slits in dirt
they rise, and here they stop.
A cold long light swings over.

Hard like ice
it cracks their shins —
they feel a drill and mallet
climb their bones, then cold
then warmth as blood spills out from pockets,
chests, and mouths.
No mother comes to help, although
a metal voice is whining
'boys, relax', as one
by one they totter to their knees.

1975

Jennifer Rankin

1941–79; b Sydney, and grew up there. She worked in a variety of clerical jobs, taught
English in secondary school, and was also a playwright. *Collected Poems* (1990).

Cicada Singing

A bird is chasing the cicada!
I see them skim over the thin grass

into the trees.

And last night cicada they nearly had you,
my skinny son and his friend,

shimmying up gumtrees in the cool dark street
coming home tired and unsuccessful.

Shall I tell them tonight
you are in that tree?

With your life expectancy
six days in the sun
eight years in the earth
and the long slow crawl behind you?

Shall I tell them tonight?

Ah! but the probing beak of the bird
prises you out!
Quick in the swift air
it is the urgent flap of bird-wind

and you glint green my cicada
in this instant-wheeling-garden
you glint green
under the weight of the bird

you glint green and the sun shines

catching itself on your newly-dried wings
that tear like a child's first transfer in the air.

1978

Sea-bundle

I carried you to an island.

A thousand years of sailing
and the reef still stretching away.

Wrapped in old sails you ate
out of my hand

you drank from the sea

you gazed ahead in the morning
returning each night.

I handled you gently in your bandages
I brought you safely to shore.

Now I squat on the sand.
It is mid-summer and I am unwrapping you.

I hold you within my hand
and you twist in the sun.

The sea spins its mirror over our heads.

Here in the sand the worn calico unravels.
I have come to the end.

You stretch and flap up into my face.
I am old and I cry into your hands.

1978

John Tranter

b 1943, Cooma, south-eastern NSW. He has worked as an editor, critic and radio producer, and lives in Sydney. *Selected Poems* (1982), *Under Berlin* (1988).

from *Crying in Early Infancy*

64

A gift to stir up fevered passions,
in a fit to envision a disastrous future
and to tell it as explicitly as possible,
to see through others as clearly as a mirror
but not to see yourself at all,
this is your basic equipment. As for the rest —
compass, map, a traveller's phrase-book —
use them only if you have need.

You have been provided with a wife and child
and a passport, and a respectable position
with a firm of publishers in the city.
As for the stammering, the occasional
failure of nerve . . . just do the best you can.
Oh — pencil, paper, one-way ticket. Have fun.

1977

A Jackeroo in Kensington

With a fistful of dollars in a knapsack
and a brutal turn of phrase, colonials
are crashing the party. *Cette parade sauvage:*
on the skyline you can see Rupert Murdoch
crawling over Fleet Street, a pigmy King Kong —
did they shrug off an empire for this?
Too right boss, that's what I want to hear,
the glib, slangy lingo of the tango dancers
steaming through the Heads in a sepia haze —
it's the bottom of the world
say the blond sophisticates. Hang on:
wasn't 'King Kong' invented in America?
The eyes that look into Australia
are European eyes, Peter Porter said, but
my friends' kids holidayed in Hollywood,
and live in San Francisco. I'm
middle-aged, and England made me, cobber,
reading Maugham in the shower recess — though
what about Malraux? and Lao Tzu?
I'm going to be a Chinaman
next time around, speaking perfect English
or Creole, who can choose between
the torrid charms of the one and the
cool, pragmatic bite of the other?
Can you say *You fuckwit!* in Italian?
No way, but if you play Wagner
loud enough you'll get rich quick
in the Bloomsbury sense of the word —
a humus of culture, a knack for sleeping in,
these things adorn you like a froth
and the National Gallery opens its doors
for you, and you alone, at last.

1982

The eyes that look . . .': a reference to Peter Porter's poem 'Talking to You Afterwards'.

Lufthansa

Flying up a valley in the Alps where the rock
rushes past like a broken diorama
I'm struck by an acute feeling of precision —
the way the wing-tips flex, just a little
as the German crew adjust the tilt of the sky and
bank us all into a minor course correction
while the turbo-props gulp at the mist
with their old-fashioned thirsty thunder — or
you notice how the hostess, perfecting a smile
as she offers you a dozen drinks, enacts what is
almost a craft: Technical Drawing, for example,
a subject where desire and function, in the hands
of a Durer, can force a thousand fine ink lines
to bite into the doubts of an epoch, spelling
Humanism. Those ice reefs repeat the motto
whispered by the snow-drifts on the north side
of the woods and model villages: the sun
has a favourite leaning, and the Nordic flaw
is a glow alcohol can fan into a flame.
And what is this truth that holds the grey
shaking metal whole while we believe in it?
The radar keeps its sweeping intermittent promises
speaking metaphysics on the phosphor screen;
our faith is sad and practical, and leads back
to our bodies, to the smile behind the drink
trolley and her white knuckles as the plane drops
a hundred feet. The sun slanting through a porthole
blitzes the ice-blocks in my glass of lemonade
and splinters light across the cabin ceiling.
No, two drinks — one for me, one for Katharina
sleeping somewhere — suddenly the Captain
lifts us up and over the final wall
explaining roads, a town, a distant lake
as a dictionary of shelter — sleeping elsewhere
under a night sky growing bright with stars.

1988

Poolside

[from *Sex Chemistry*]

The host climbs out, soaked and spitting oaths,
and a teenage girl leaves the barbecue.
Two of those drinks your wife mixed,
bright pink and cheerful, and I'm
seeing double: breasts, twin headaches

exactly the same size await me
frowning from each temple, and a diptych
concusses the chatter: a car salesman
hitting his better half. A pygmy politics emerges
wherever two or more of you are gathered,
shopping together. All right, stop biting,
I'd much rather sleep with you than with
that other poltergeist. You're greedy,
aren't you? O Painted Laugh, why is your
belly convulsing? Can 'a man' become a sign
for 'a muscular spasm'? Horoscope,
betray yourself, take me back to a feast,
if this is a feast, these glib flirtations,
the whole gang badly knocked out
by the mundane speech the flame attempts,
each sleep a cancelled cheque, as I
watch myself thinking of you, deracinated
Sweetheart, boarding a Greyhound.

1988

Crosstalk

[from *Sex Chemistry*]

The way you lie there, it's an opinion, those
bronze medal limbs, the sheets crumpled,
your body the site and centre of conspicuous
waste. It's a vote against the mob,
the way you flick the lamp out, thoughts
akimbo, and stare at the visual display.
Sleep, says the computer.

It sounds brilliant in the dark, at 2 a.m., that
breathing in stereo, so crisp, or rain
in the mesh grille of a microphone.
Is it recording a storm, or sound effects?
The machine listens to its own astrology. Who
left the screen on? That red, that luminescent
green, I must be sleepwalking. Toast,

ham and eggs for two, all on the video.
Does a wish flicker, like that?
Then you disappear leaving a faint ghost
and go to black, as the program dumps
a bracelet of digits in the outboard memory.
The printout spelling doom, do you carry it
with you through sleep, a gift, a poison?

And when you wake at sunrise, heavy breather,
golden in the light, will you be content?
Hush — the shower's whispering, breakfast is ready,
and two expensive German microphones wait for
breath, for movement, for the trace of your desire.

1988

South Coast after Rain, 1960

1

The clouds have drifted back to the hills
and the late afternoon sun spills onto the town
lighting up a steeple and a sign advertising
    diesel fuel.

2

In a back paddock two men
are loading a pile of drums
slowly onto an old green truck.

3

A car hurries along the road
in the distance — you can just hear it —
a teenager driving his dad's new Holden
to meet the prettiest girl in town.

4

Nightfall: the lights go on
outside the picture theatre. A gang of boys
hang around the Red Rose Café
    smoking cigarettes.

They watch a car pass
and turn at the end of the street
where the bridge points over the black water
towards the future. They watch it
    drive back.

5

Ah, the girl, how lovely she is;
at sixteen, how grown up.
He thinks of meeting her in twenty minutes,
    nothing else.

The radio glows in the dashboard,
the rock'n'roll sounds brand new.
Things will be like this
    forever.

6

I see them meet,
they fight, they separate,
travel,
 grow old.

7

The truck door slams.
One of the men opens a cold bottle.
Outside the cinema the weeds push up
 through the footpath.

8

Parked in the darkened driveway
they sink into a kiss.
    The radio
fills the car with emotion.

             1988

Robert Adamson

b 1943, Sydney; left school at thirteen. He has been influential both as a poetry editor and as an organizer of public readings. He lives in Sydney. *Selected Poems* (1990).

Dead Horse Bay

Quick hands on spinning ropes
at dawn, blood rising
to the jumping cords.

Ice-pack over bad burns
and the catfish venom.
Rock salt against gut-slime.

A southerly blowing up
on the full tide, nets
in mud and mesh-gutting snags.

The bread tasting
like kero-sponge, crazed gulls
crashing onto the stern.

Mullet at 3 cents a pound
by the time sun hits
the bar of the *Angler's Rest*.

Get drunk enough to keep at it,
clean the gear for tonight
and another bash.

Remember that night in '68
how we killed 'em
right through the month

couldn't have gone wrong,
so thick you could've
walked over the water.

When the bream are running
like that, nothing can touch you
and everything matters

and you don't want 'em to stop
and you can't slow down
you can't imagine.

                                        1977

Into Forest

My face the long grey fish drifts above
the soft floor over the leaves
returning to their previous lives once more

it looks into the centre of seed pods
ripe in the fern-trees with eyes trying to forget
High above where I have never lived

a thornbill jets through the twigs
and the rufous whistlers begin their territorial
alarms — So finally I am here

watching my face searching for the next mask

In the house my wife is moving behind
sheets of glass holding the pages of sleep
I cannot read — she waits for

the time we have been trying for
the moments without wings we can never own
she looks out at my face

it is a life I am unable to recall or imagine

In the house among the spotted gums
my face has been up all night speaking of itself
speaking in tongues

crashing about in the living room
a bower bird caged in growing weak

in panic howling through the domestic light

Here in the bush it makes no sound
the eyes join the moving sky
and the mouth draws in new air for its lies

the black tongue a broken wing
and the beak nose a dorsal before the chin's bristle

I try to remember a face in a language
we speak trees in

1982

Dreaming Up Mother

Understanding is all, my mother would tell me,
and then walk away from the water;

Understanding is nothing I think, as I mumble
embellished phrases of what's left of her story.

Though I keep battering myself against sky,
throwing my body into the open day.

Landscapes are to look at, they taught me,
but now the last of the relatives are dead.

Where do these walks by the shore take us
she would say, wanting to clean up,

after the picnic, after the nonsense.
I have been a bother all the years from my birth.

Look out — the river pulls through the day
and Understanding like a flaming cloud, goes by.

1988

144

Caroline Caddy

b 1944, WA; early childhood in USA. She has worked in Road Dental Units throughout WA, and she farms on the state's south coast. *Letters from the North* (1985), *Beach Plastic* (1989).

Letters from the North

i

The ships come and the ships go
but we are getting nowhere.
The YANKS have banned our welder as incompetent.
'Mind you son
we're not saying
he doesnt know his job —
we just think
he is
incompetent.'

They're funny with their one arm waving GO WEST YOUNG MAN
and the other pledging allegiance to THE CORPORATION.

I want you to know what it's like up here.
I'm writing so you'll know
despite everything.

The colors are red and blue.
Everywhere you look is half red and half blue.
Blue sky and red earth or blue sea and red almost purple sky
when they are loading.

The dust is a trap.
It gives the illusion of rich brown loam
but it's only finely weathered iron ore.

ii

I am watching twelve backs with twelve different tans.
It is six in the morning.
By eleven the rail will be impossible to handle.
There is one cloud in the sky   pink of course
from the dust.

Tino arrived yesterday —
no jack   no spare   blows a tyre
hitches into camp   borrows the ute
blows another tyre —
He's brought his wife up with him.
She doesn't speak a word of english.

I'm not sure what you want to hear.
It's difficult to describe the land we're working through.
Sometimes there is only heat sometimes only wind.
I have stopped expecting definite rivers or mountains.

iii

The YANKS in their SUPERVISORY CAPACITY
say the track has to be moved   again
and they are GODS   up here and their WORD IS LAW
so I listen.
They are convinced ten words say ten times more than one
so I listen some more.
Then Tino walks up and listens too.
Tino listens with his whole face   his hands
his body and his feet.
Tino can keep them talking for hours by listening.
Tino listens them into agreeing not to move the track.

It's the middle of the bloody night.
I wait to flag down a train.
There's a brilliant lightning display in the east —
no sound   just a constant glow brighter and weaker.
I feel as if something tremendous is going on over there
but I'm not close enough to see.

iv

Today we worked for six hours then chucked it in.
The sleepers are treated for white ants —
some creosote ammonia stuff.
In this heat the fumes really knock you about.

Tino rolled up late.
I've got to go with him he says.
His wife wont talk to him
and the woman next door hears her crying all day.
We get there and she wont let Tino in
only me with my stock-phrase Italian.
Bella   Bella   come sta? I say
and she's crying in her black Calabrian dress
and she's crying in her black Calabrian headscarf
and she's crying in her black Calabrian shoes and stockings
and she wants to go home   she wants to go home.
So we let Tino in
and we drink wine and eat cake   eat cake and drink wine.
Then we put her on the plane to Perth.
Tino says his family will look after her.

It's been raining thirty miles away.
The road is closed at Cane River.
Nothing is getting through.

v

I want to tell you about the machines.
They are like big animals hoisting themselves along.
They grip the rail with huge pincers and lift it.
When the tamping rods go deep into the ballast
the ground feels like it's trying to get up.
The noise they make
keeps everything out.

vi

The camp is overcrowded.
There's a strike on.
The men are bored and brawling over trifles.

It seems the CORPORATION'S been caught short.
The Japs are cutting back on orders.
Eighty miles of track   a new harbour and loading gear —
there's talk of putting it all in mothballs
and the usual theories on who's to blame.

There is little time to think.
Even when we are not working
the heat wont allow.
All your letters have come at once.

vii

Port Hedland is a dirty place.
Rubbish everywhere.
No one cares.

Last night I find a drunken Gin in the ute.
She says I'm her darling and she wants some money.
I boot her out.
Next morning I find she's pinched the radio.

viii

There's been an accident.
Tino —   crushed between a low loader
and a stack of sleepers
and we've only got the ute to get him to Tom Price.
Forty miles of gravel and the shockers in the ute have gone.
Sometimes this place gives me the shits.

ix

It's raining. The camp's a pig-sty.
The job has slowed by miles.

The YANKS are getting themselves freighted out   free
if they can produce certificates stating they are unfit
for this climate —
'Mind you son
you'll have to get
your butts in gear —
not that we
dont think
you cant
do it.'
Which means we can call our mistakes our own now.

x

There's no map I can send to show you
exactly where we are.
The earth is the same red
the sky the same blue   deeper though
cleaner I guess   from the rain.

Three hundred yards each side of the track is untouched
but you'd swear it had been mined already.
The hills are bulldozed ore dumps.
The plants look like they've barely grown back.
I'm stunned over and over
that it's all quite natural.

1985

Hal Colebatch

b 1945, Perth. He works as a solicitor, publisher and journalist in Perth. *Outer Charting* (1985).

Third Song of Popeye the Sailorman

Sun and clear air today as I scrape
the barnacles from this beached boat's hull.
Singing because my heart is full,
no longer searching now to find escape.
Such small things can fill the heart — a letter
that makes no promises, and yet reminds one
of things too long forgotten. A tentative hand,
a few well-chosen words. This day is better
at last because of small things. The sun
fires the river, the water laps the sand
limpid and bright. I sing at my scraper,
warm in my shorts, under the boat's red side.
Transparent shrimps quest the lip of the tide.
Nothing is promised. Nothing on paper.

1979

Visiting Dachau, 1973

A squirrel runs between two oak trees,
the air holds soft, almost invisibly falling rain.
Seeing me lost, two bright girls give me
a lift back to the train.

They ask me about Australia. I answer,
hunched with my pack in the Volkswagen's front seat.
They point to churches, and other places of interest
in each quiet street.

They are busy with youth work. I know little first hand
of Australian youth work by churches. Still I say
what I can of such matters. Soft evening descends
on cool, near-shadowless day.

Evening lights small leaves of early spring,
old houses, a castle tall on a hill.
We share some drinks at the railway station kiosk.
The rain-washed air is still.

Small leaves are palest green in quiet dusk
against pale grey. We drink, the bill is paid.
I thank them for their kindness and board the train
with a souvenir bottle of lemonade.

1985

Robert Gray

b 1945, Coffs Harbour, NSW north coast. He has worked in advertising and as a bookshop
assistant in Sydney, where he lives. *Selected Poems* (rev. edn, 1990).

The Meatworks

Most of them worked around the slaughtering
out the back, where concrete gutters
crawled off
heavily, and the hot, fertilizer-thick,
sticky stench of blood
sent flies mad,
but I settled for one of the lowest-paid jobs, making mince
right the furthest end from those bellowing,
sloppy yards. Outside, the pigs' fear
made them mount one another
at the last minute. I stood all day
by a shaking metal box
that had a chute in, and a spout,
snatching steaks from a bin they kept refilling
pushing them through
arm-thick corkscrews, grinding around inside it, meat or not —
chomping, bloody mouth —
using a greasy stick
shaped into a penis.
When I grabbed it the first time
it slipped, slippery as soap, out of my hand,
in the machine
that gnawed it hysterically a few moments
louder and louder, then, shuddering, stopped;
fused every light in the shop.
Too soon to sack me —
it was the first thing I'd done.
For a while, I had to lug gutted pigs
white as swedes
and with straight stick tails
to the ice rooms, hang them by the hooves
on hooks — their dripping

solidified like candle-wax — or pack a long intestine
with sausage meat.
We got meat to take home —
bags of blood;
red plastic with the fat showing through.
We'd wash, then
out on the blue metal
towards town; but after sticking your hands all day
in snail-sheened flesh,
you found, around the nails, there was still blood.
I didn't usually take the meat.
I'd walk home on
the shiny, white-bruising beach, in mauve light,
past the town.
The beach, and those startling, storm-cloud mountains, high
beyond the furthest fibro houses, I'd come
to be with. (The only work
was at this Works.) — My wife
carried her sandals, in the sand and beach grass,
to meet me. I'd scoop up shell-grit
and scrub my hands,
treading about
through the icy ledges of the surf
as she came along. We said that working with meat was like
burning-off the live bush
and fertilizing with rottenness,
for this frail green money.
There was a flaw to the analogy
you felt, but one
I didn't look at, then —
the way those pigs stuck there, clinging onto each other.

1973

Late Ferry

The late ferry is leaving now;
I stay to watch
from the balcony, as it goes up onto
the huge dark harbour,

out beyond that narrow wood jetty;
the palm tree tops
make a sound like touches
of the brush on a snare drum

in the windy night. Going beyond
street lights' fluorescence

over the dark water, a ceaseless
activity, like chromosomes

uniting and dividing. And out beyond
the tomato stake patch
of the yachts, with their orange
lights; leaving this tuberous

small bay, for the city
across an empty dark. There, neon
redness trembles down in the water
as if into ice, and

the longer white lights
feel nervously about in the blackness,
towards here, like hands
after the light switch.

The ferry wades now into the broad
open harbour, to be lost soon
amongst a silver blizzard of light
swarming below the Bridge:

a Busby Berkeley spectacular
with thousands in frenzied, far-off
choreography, in their silver lamé,
the Bridge like a giant prop.

One does seem in a movie theatre:
that boat is small as a moth
wandering through the projector's beam,
seeing it float beneath the city.

I'll lose sight of the ferry soon —
I can see it while it's on darkness,
and it looks like honeycomb,
filled as it is with its yellow light.

1978

Bondi

The waves are a shoal of white fins, in the end of every downhill street,
and along the streets are stacked blunt-faced blocks of flats:
big, plastery, peeling buildings, in cream, with art deco curves and angles.
Behind this, for a thousand acres, the buckled suburbs of dark brick.
Curtains trail outwards on the heat, and a smell of gas leaks,
above singed grass in tiny yards, grey palings, chlorine-blue hydrangeas,
gas pipes like creepers over walls.

There are garbage bins left lying about, empty milk bottles on marble steps,
always snail-dribble across the concrete, to the crushed snail shells.
The sun trundles around and around, amongst its flapping fire.
In the longest street, out toward the cave-in on the headland, is a children's park,
where, through empty swings, with their oversized hot chains, the surf
     swings.
Out here are callow home units of pale brick, fenestrated as that rock face
below the cliff's edge they're built upon.
Beyond a last railing, the sea throws over and spreads its crocheted cloth
across the rock table, and (something you can't watch for long — it is like
     madness)
draws it off once again.
Around at the beach-front, rattling fun parlours, discos and milkbars, the
     sign-painting
lurid as tattoos, thickly over them.
Cars are tilted along all the gutters, strung together closely as caterpillars,
in the colours of children's sweets. The grit settles, coating
windscreens and duco; vinyl seats bake in the sun,
and that smell will sicken the overwrought children in the late afternoon,
     going home.
All day these headlands lie spread apart to the pleasurable, treacherous
     elements.
The place seems scoured by weather of every other ideal.
But then, a white yacht will appear in the ultramarine passage, an icon
of perfect adaptation, and the people along the sand,
as though in a grandstand, or those wading out
through the low waves towards it, seem all of them everywhere over this
like walking moths, that fan its easy passage with their wings.
It goes wandering on midway in the spectrum of blue before them, in the
     garment of serenity.
This is the only sort of vision we shall have, and it costs money,
and therefore Bondi is lying crammed together, obtuse, with barely a tree,
     behind us —
Every cent is firstly for the secure mechanisms of comfort.
It is not pleasure, to be exact, but its appropriation. And not mindlessness,
     but the mind.
For at the beach, so much that is nature can be seen to have been called
into the one procession of decay. Flesh become crude and brief
as figures shaped out of beach sand. So many of these people
look as though used like Bondi grit, with its scraps and butts and matchsticks.
Still, the young girls are loping on the sea-front, who secretly
amaze themselves with an easy skill they've found —
who can swing their breasts and all the shapes that are surging on their
     bodies
as if the drum majorettes for this parade.
At dusk, the parking spaces above the sea have emptied
and sand blows along the bitumen like smoke.

The garbage bins on posts are steep in their slipping litter.
And the gulls, that run and screech and scatter each other amongst it,
    never make
contented noises — are scrabbling constantly;
only sometimes one of them is carried off by the wind, down the bay,
    and it goes along
on its outriggers, smoothly; beautiful, particularly in the dusk,
when it flows away as smoothly, sideways, as the running shallows —
its whiteness, that is picked up by the whiteness of a wave's single wingbeat
out there on the deep-mauve water, creating a vast space.

1983

The Lake

open
screendoor

seashells

wireless
murmur

bathroom
water

louvres

ballooning
light

1988

Mark O'Connor

---

b 1945, Ararat, western Victoria. A noted environmentalist who has lived in many parts
of the country, he has been a full-time poet since 1973 and is now based in Canberra.
The Great Forest (1989), *Fire-stick Farming* (1990).

Turtles Hatching

Waiting for weeks till the last one is ready to run, they

break through to twilight: the life-race is on.
Winds and oceans that call give no order but one:
'Downhill, fast; when you hit water, swim.' Last

will be picked; so will first. One in a hundred survives.
So they break sand & run, downhill as if cursed. (Seagulls
halloo joy, ghost-crabs skitter out.) They are high-revving toys

each wound for his chance. The course is uncertain,
ten sandy yards to cool foam, or half of a low-tide mile
over pits and castles of rock-crab, every hole an abyss,

every cross-ridge a death-lane; unable to stop,
indifferent whether scrambling in sand, scrabbling in slime,
or sculling deluded through sand-pools to beaches of death.

Caught in cracks they push hard down the crab's throat,
still punting on while life lasts, in search of the dark
and lovely reef water, the splash in the in-walled ear.

Their limbs have no setting but *go*. Friendly and clean,
with their leathery touch in the palm, likeable
as a dry handshake, a childish pleasure to handle, determined

as cats; this driving downhill force that will reach,
tourist, twice the mass of your coffin, yet weigh,
till it comes ashore, not a gram.

Tweaks the heart, though, to see them seek fate in a crab-hole.
I pulled one out once, wedged and still struggling
down, dropped it with a jerk — a great horny claw

like a parrot's beak had crushed the midsection, sheared
off the head, and behind moved the armoured tarantula legs
of a hairy scuttler with lobe-stalked eyes.

In pity I gathered a living brother, hiked it over the rock-flats,
(fighting on in my hand) while its brethren, obedient,
filed along moonless crevices, sating ambuscades of queued-up crabs,

laid it down on a rock slope, a foot from the water. It flopped
on straight for its freedom, tripped over a two-inch ledge —
fell and rocked on its back. (A crab darted out, saw my shadow, back-

sidled to shadow.) It squirmed and righted itself, hurried
on (since Nature has taught them to fear no predator
but time, no approach will deflect them), found the slight wash of

a ripple and lost half its weight; then, re-stranded, pressed on, met
the incoming surf of a wavelet, capsized, scrambled up, then
plugged on, hit new surf and breasted it well; turned its

flippers to sculling, still floating, too light to submerge;
spiralled a clumsy provocative line, spinnering out
to the moon, lucky with absent sharks and gentle water.

Slipping in, as it left, the shadow, a thousand times larger,
of a parent come shoreward to lay; two ends of the earthbound process
linked in the uncomprehending meeting of kin.

As the small shadow pedalled and bobbed, the great one wavered and slid;
for a second the greater obscured the lesser, then as surely
slid on; and the lesser was gone.

1980

Minnamurra Forest

Rainforest is a symphony, never graspable in full,
replete with fugitive notes
and familiar themes pursued
with a soft nutrient harmony.

Trees dwarf the birds
like midges in their boughs
but to the ear it's all reversed —
the leaves' mist-like murmuring flits, a furtive sigh
among sun-splashed columns of birdsong.

High on the cliff
the warm steam trailing unobscures a tree so high
you thought up there was only cloud.
Creepers rise in diminished coils, like smoke
to tether a drifting cloud of leaves.

The Red Cedar's light bunched-green
lace skirt swirled out
above its shingle bark, with one basket fern
perched akimbo on a bent high elbow,
might take a millennium of Chinese art to formalise.
Here it was found and cut.

The brown torrent bludgeoning down
like some huge expensive unstoppable machine,
a vibrating ladder of rock, foam, sticks,
will turn off in a million years
when its cliff is gone.

Elsewhere the bio-sphere
is paper-thin, a waxed green blade thrust out
into the solar glare. Here
it's a hundred feet of fertile greening gloom.

On the cliffside a harness of creepers
reins back the reared bulk of a churnwood trunk.
Each leaf falls lightly as a sparrow
and is recycled skilfully.
While tons of hardwood poise above your head
a millipede ripples from one leaf-side to another . . .

1989

The Jigsaw Woman

(Children's Museum, Melbourne 1988)

The three-dimensional jigsaw woman
invites you to put in a Thumb
and pull out a Lung.

The jigsaw woman has hard
plastic organs that click
and fit. Her Liver clips
around the Spleen.

A child would win the race
to rebuild her in two minutes,
with a bit left over. The plump grub
in the Womb fascinates:
'Careful! — don't drop the baby!'

A surgeon last year perfected
use of the one-dollar zipper
for recurrent operations.
The jigsaw person approves. Someday
there may be a right of self-access
— a boon to the Soapie writers: *Frowning,*
J.T. butts his cigar, unzips, pulls out his spleen,
says: 'Just as I thought. Off-colour.'
Or *Mary Lou: 'Of course I'm pregnant, see for yourself! . . .'*
— *'If the Court please . . . Your Honor . . .'*

Unscrew the breast-plate:
the glabrous simplicity
fashionable since Greece
lifts off. Beneath: a mass of squirming complexity
fixed, gorgon-style, in polyurethane.
The Breast Glands, stripped
of the smooth flesh-bra,
prove convoluted as the Brain,
an eroded fissured dome
with flaccid cupola on top.

The embossed Heart, worn jauntily off centre,
is meshed in a map of its own vessels,
forking and delta-ing,
unknown Amazon.
Muscle-sheets suspend the Womb's closed hammock;
the Poo Canal winds close behind.
Her lower lips part smoothly, vertical,
in a lifetime's cautious invitation.

The Lungs' mahogany feeds the Aorta
where an artery branches back, brimming crimson,
to the Heart: full priority
to Management Services.

The left Lung, smaller, leaves room for its pump
identically in sheep and humans; all babies learn
the squelchy tom-tom of a close-up Heart.
The big Bertha of the Left Ventricle
jutting against the Breast Bone
taps out the standard off-beat,
since mimicked in our clocks.

**

Not so the real organs,
in formalin. Beneath the skin
seethes ultimate functionalism
with nothing labelled.
The Lung's tough blood-bag
is no light sponge-rubber sack
but a controlled froth of gas and fluid,
delicate go-between
to mix blood with its clotting enemy.
The Small Intestine's clammy python
slops and flops, no rigid loops to snap inside
the Large Intestine's donut,
but a wet-sludge extraction-works
valved and filtered.

A subtle chamois drapes
the hand-bones' strings and levers; plump skin
makes of the face a signal-screen
that dissected seems all scaffolding,
a scoreboard from behind.
No bright liveries for the body's members
but a nightscape of pink and watery masses
from Pia Mater to Corpus Cavernosum. Deft pilots

in these waters thread the Straits
of Labbé, have mapped the Glabella,
rounded the Pons, the Fornix, and passed
the weeping Islets of Langerhans
— *All straits, and none but straits.* Blindfold,
they'd know the Tongue's thick nobbled doormat,
the Brain's soft ripple of matter.

And this sea's archipelagoes
multiply likenesses:
the convolutions of the Ear
are echoed in Vagina;
the kidney shape of Womb
repeats in Testicle; there is similar habitat
in the broad swamplands of Liver-'n-Lungs
and the Corpus Spongium of the Membrum Virile.
Corrugations of Intestine wall
dumbly mimic the Cerebellum's lining,
the whole unpredicted and inescapable
as the map of a new continent,
each fjord or plateau
simply how things are,
and were not known before.

[1990]

Diane Fahey

b 1945, Melbourne; moved to Adelaide 1985. She has worked as a teacher in secondary and tertiary education, and is now a full-time writer. *Metamorphoses* (1988), *Turning the Hourglass* (1990).

Eileithyia

Eileithyia, goddess of birth,
has seen much death.
Calliope says, consoling her,
that all is metaphor —
that birth and death
are so woven together
who can tell them apart?

The death-god is no poet.
Single-minded, almost pedantic,
'You take the metaphors,
I'll take the facts,' he says.

Calliope: ancient Greek muse of epic poetry.

Eileithyia responds
with silence, feeling
the power inside her hands
which, again and again,
pull life from life,
slapping it into breath,
cradling it into comfort.

Through the turning point
of an afternoon, she walks
across a field of wheat —
a lake of fire — holding
at her centre the memory
of each lost, each future
life. She carries that
weight, that lightness,
into shadowed sunlight,
alive and herself
in the wholeness,
      the brokenness,
      of now, of here.

1988

Remembering Ophelia

1

Blood trickles down from the castle
filling the flowers that fill her eyes.

2

Confused, and the victim of confusion . . .
How water clarifies the mind.

3

As they lay littering the hall in their blood
she lingered in crumbling masonry and pillars,
in weeds and flowers intermarrying outside the walls.

4

Centuries later, she returned with a film crew.
She was wearing jeans, an Indian shirt covered
with flowers and a head scarf.
                              He was still
lying there among the others with their sprawling
limbs and broken swords.
                              After the filming,
she took off her badge and pinned it to his chest

— 'Take the Toys from the Boys,' it read — then left
without a farewell kiss, though she was compassionate,
and over the bitterness by now.

5

He wasn't mad because he knew he was mad.
She was mad because she didn't.
That's why *he* knew when he was dying,
but *she* didn't.
                    Did she know he wasn't mad?
No, because she couldn't.
                    Did he know she was mad?
— 'Madam, I never think of such things!'

6

Invisible rape.
He had penetrated
and withdrawn
without laying
a finger on her.
You wouldn't
find it in any
statute book . . .
It made her think
the real thing
must be awful.
Sometimes, she
laughed and cried
for hours, but
mostly there
was her sewing
now; and she
fiddled a lot
with her shawl.

7

He died surrounded by enemies who were really
friends who were really enemies etcetera.
She died alone. But up on the hill
were autumn hedges full of leaves,
birds' eyes, and knots of wood,
all watching.

8

The rats were leaving the castle,
grey drops sliding down escarpments —
prelude to some final loneliness.

9

She was surprised when they asked her to do
the flowers for the funeral — such an outsider
in her bare, small plot against the wall.
'I suppose they like everyone to be involved,'
she thought, and agreed. It was a grand
State Funeral, of course, with a huge monument
plumb in the middle of consecrated ground.
She decided on violets, daisies, rue — all
her old favorites.
                              Strange, he had never liked
flowers. 'Such frail things,' he'd winced,
'so ephemeral, so easily crushed . . . *like you*,'
he'd added with a sneer. 'Oh, we're all mortal,'
she'd replied, 'and anyway, *I'm* not afraid of ghosts!'
(She could stand up to him in those days.)
And how apt her words . . . Death had come for them
both, soon afterwards; and now she was a ghost,
and saw how natural it was, knew she'd been
perfectly right not to be frightened.

10

How could Ophelia, still in the mermaid state,
drown? On a bank of the river she combed her hair,
refreshed after her swim. A humble fisherman,
passing by, conceived an immortal love for her . . .
Merciful, she gave him a smile, and a nice big kiss,
and sent him home.

11

She could remember him much younger,
muscular chest and loins straining
through leather as he whispered,
'God, Ophelia, you're a real turn on!'

Her Mum had said, 'Just keep your
distance for a while,' then,
with a wink and a smile, 'They get like
that sometimes — he'll get over it!'

Next, he had gone away to College,
and come back. ('A real *hinterlectewal*,'
sneered her Dad.) One day,
she met him in the High Street.

There was a long silence, then
she said, 'Funny world, isn't it?'

'Rotten,' he snapped, and walked on.
He's just not interested, she thought,

just as I'm getting to be,
with all those fantasies of kissing,
and fondling, and swimming
naked in the river.

12

'It's not polite to leave the world without saying goodbye.'
That's what they told her on the Other Side, and sent her back.
Now she's a florist in Kensington. She's got to know the world
a bit better this time round, and is almost ready to say hello.

1990

Dressmaker

As a girl I loved fabrics, stitching and moulding them
to fit. I remember a flared dress, pink roses on white.
Wearing it with my first high heels, I tottered past
neighbourhood louts slung on a verandah; from their transistor
Marty Robbins sang 'A White Sport Coat and a Pink Carnation'.
As I blushed, they eyed the smoky summer air.
                                              At sixteen,
a slippery silk dress with whorls of red and crimson,
pinched in with a cummerbund. With unswerving hips
I passed the greengrocer, an Italian who sighed, whistled,
called in one sound, his pregnant wife thrusting beans
and tomatoes into brown paper bags; her look touched mine:
wary, beyond challenge, sisterly.
                                  Ten years of illness next,
when I bundled myself inside coats in summer, wore black
as often as not. Hard to stand straight inside a body
so out of kilter.
                  Since then I have put on the garment
of my womanhood. It marks the curves and leanings
of my flesh, holds in, reveals, what I have come to be,
beyond promise and blight. I know its weight, its transparency,
its rawness, its flawed smoothness. I wear it now
with something close to ease, with the freedom, almost,
of nakedness.

1990

Rhyll McMaster

b 1947, Brisbane. She farms at Braidwood, south-eastern NSW. *The Brineshrimp* (1972), *Washing the Money* (1986).

Birds

I listen at night to birds
resettling on branches,
shifting on leaves and twigs with bone feet.
Asleep in our trees, padded around us,
they breathe through their beaks;
their brains tick over.

One afternoon by the pond
two Welcome swallows
whipped past our heads like Ninja stars,
then sheared up the hill looking over their shoulders;
Insects and birds cloud the sky.

At dusk the birds
slit the night air like darts.
We track them with field glasses;
You see their plumage, I watch their eyes.

Once I caught a crow
looking straight at me.
Its eye shone like a man's
dressed in a bird suit.
Breathing, it lifted its neck feathers
and screamed;
its brain ticked over.

At night I listen to birds sleeping.
Puffed out like dust balls their odour is heavy.
I dream of their grey skin
the juicy growth of their quills.
I smell the hotness under their wings,
feel their crushable bodies
that fit into the hand.

1972

A Dream of Washed Hair

Standing under the shower
my mother washes her hair;
she is small and young.

She slicks back her hair from the temples
with the palm of one hand.
Her skin looks secret and cool;
her life does not go on from here.

Though she dresses and goes
this I don't see in my dream;
she leans and smiles.
She is not thinking of me
though I stare in her eyes.
She is thinking of nothing at all
in that water, this dream, that stopped world.

1986

Peter Kocan

b 1947, Newcastle, NSW; childhood in Melbourne. He spent ten years from 1966 in a psychiatric institution in NSW. Also a novelist, he lives at Tuggerawong, NSW central coast. *Armistice* (1980), *Freedom to Breathe* (1985).

from *The Private Poems of Governor Caulfield*

O'Shaughnessy

A rebel of Ninety Eight
He disdained that defeat,
Fled his lean village, took
To the hills, a one-man outbreak.

Captured and sentenced to hang
He invited the judge along
'To learn the ropes for when
It's Your Honour's own turn!'

One of officialdom's brief
Whims commuted this to Life
In New South Wales. On the ship
He tore the decking up,

Urged mutiny. Later
He broke from Parramatta,
Faced muskets with a blunt hoe
At the Rouse Hill fiasco.

Governor Caulfield: a fictional figure.

The painstaking tuition
Of Norfolk taught him caution
Only. In time he came back
In irons, to break rock,

And had almost got away
When bullets smashed his knees. Today
They came off. Useless
Of course — the gangrene was

Too ripe.
          Now the body, tied
On the table in a hack of blood,
Is the mere shed chain of a man
Triumphantly on the run.

[I recognize it now as plain report]

I recognize it now as plain report,
The factual depiction of a scene
By Matthew and by Mark and Luke and John.
All my life I'd vaguely imagined it

As something like poetic metaphor,
An antique fable, an allegory
That you grow up with and only half-see
In stained glass through the peculiar air

Inside a church. But this country's harsh light;
The desert-tasting wind that rushes past;
The stony, thorny places; the dry dust;
Seem almost perfectly to recreate

The setting: *Del Espiritu Santo*.
And here we see it happen, see it all —
The poor man in a humble apparel
Stripped for his accusers. We see him go

To be scourged by soldiers. And in his bonds
We see him taken to his public death.
And I see myself, a governor with
A faint, distressing urge to wash my hands.

[1982]

Del Espiritu Santo: Australia del Espiritu Santo ('South Land of the Holy Spirit') was the name given
to Vanuatu by the Portuguese navigator Pedro de Quiros during his expedition of 1606 in search of
a southern continent.

John A. Scott

b 1948, Sussex, UK; arrived in Melbourne 1959, where he worked as a scriptwriter and teacher in media studies. He teaches writing at the University of Wollongong. *Singles* (1989), *St Clair* and *Translation* (1990).

Pride of Erin

[from *After the Dance*]

The public telephone is a cage for the exhibition
    of Chrissie.
She comes from Science to the shop.
Saunters with her friends through a suburb of dogs,
    keeping ahead of evening, just beating it inside.
Smoke from the slow-combustion heaters.
A sun, low in the sky, giving lamplight and no warmth.
A dying star and the domino theory of barking, when
    light starts to fail.
She has trouble with the door; with instructions.
Is afraid of losing her coin; doesn't have another one
    on her right now.
Is afraid of *not at home. Might be round at Greg's.*
And outside, Sharon and Cheryl and Debbie are wearing
    duffle coats, in range.
She is a carrier of nomadic truth.
Wishes commitment.
Knows of energies deep within her, under pressure, that
    she squanders on choir or keeping things clean.
No-one guesses them.
They are efforts of will.
Soldiers win medals with them.
She watches the duffle coats picking at dusk.
Watches the way teenage girls jostle and shift; are
    non-committal, like baboons.
Can't stop herself being like this most times.
Finds herself doing it.
Wonders if noticing things is the essence of growing
    old; and that as we pass some mid-point they fall
    away again, eventually back to nothing.
With difficulty, she comes from the booth into what
    is left of today.
Makes her turn.
Watches her friends move on.
In the darkness they seem to float, like objects
    displacing their own weight in water.

1984

Man in Petersham

He's dropped his heart!
His heart has fallen to the footpath.
But no-one seems surprised and least of all
the office girl whose stockings violin
across this empty road. He's dropped his heart!
It surely must be this and not his cigarettes.
The way he stares so long and makes no effort
to redeem it. And his suit is an immaculate grey,
and his shoes a duco white. And his feet are
frozen in the tiny refrigerators of his shoes.
With all the colours running out, he stares
upon his fallen heart. His mild-blue heart
shattered in its twenty filtered pieces.

1989

'Changing Room'

The breath's slow
drum-brush marks the end of Gillian's time.
Her hair's haphazard marathon, swaying
with the slowest jazz of afternoon. Detectives
wandering at her breast; the nipple's darker trilby.
A black thief hair, returning to its crime.

*

Now, amongst the sheets, there is
a trace of blacker hair, curled and blunt
as shorthand. I watch her move, the blankets
fanned across the mattress like a deal of cards.
Her foot beside an ashtray shell, its butted
cigarettes settled into parquetry. She dresses
as a child might in a changing room, all
half-under things. And what she'll do tonight
comes out of silence like a talking in her sleep.
She's leaving; and the similes are gone.
A borrowed room, and everything quite suddenly
and only like itself: this coat, this coat.
This floor, this floor.

1989

Michael Dransfield

1948-73; b Sydney. He worked briefly in the public service, then led an itinerant life in NSW. A prolific poet in his early twenties, he died of complications from drug addiction and a road injury. *Collected Poems* (1987).

Fix

It is waking in the night,
after the theatres and before the milkman,
alerted by some signal from the golden drug tapeworm
that eats your flesh and drinks your peace;
you reach for the needle and busy yourself
preparing the utopia substance in a blackened
spoon held in candle flame
by now your thumb and finger are leathery
being so often burned this way
it hurts much less than withdrawal and the hand
is needed for little else now anyway.
Then cordon off the arm with a belt,
probe for a vein, send the dream-transfusion out
on a voyage among your body machinery. Hits you like sleep —
sweet, illusory, fast, with a semblance of forever.
For a while the fires die down in you,
until you die down in the fires.
Once you have become a drug addict
you will never want to be anything else.

1970

A Strange Bird

it is a strange bird
this world

whose habit is
to fight itself

whose left wing
and right wing

tear themselves
bitterly apart

both on the side
of justice and violence

and whose great beak
gobbles the poor

1980

Alan Wearne

b 1948, Melbourne, and lives there. He has worked as an emergency teacher and as a bookshop assistant. *New Devil, New Parish* (1976), *The Nightmarkets* (1986).

from *The Nightmarkets*

It's five hundred miles.
Five hundred. To hear words. I've better things to do.
   Won't do them. Five hundred better things than words,
      to travel to words:
         Adelaide /
party / conference / alternative delegate / candidate /

         the up-and-coming
Comrade Robert Metcalfe / the love-ly Bob, the lad,
   the boy, the candy kid, the Eastern Suburbs'
      what? Man most likely to —
         what?   I'm told:
'To knock off the greasy, you know, slobbermouth, shitforbrains!'

         Ohh, my opponent:
Paul Edward Wiltshire Davison, QC, MP,
   The Honourable Member for O'Dowd: *their* lad,
      slightly ageing boy, who
         once, told me,
'What, *you*'ve got it bad? I'd swap half my wretched committee.

         Nag nag nag nag nag.
'Mate,' he boomed, 'I, unlike you, know the system works
   but I, I won't construct mental parthenons
      to private enterprise
         (as some would).
I mean, some would have me hoot off odes to business all year.

         Rotary, Lions,
   when in doubt send in Davo. He's good for gags. A port?'
   Quite a night, he and 'Snooks' having us round, but,
      in all, a bit too much
         protesting?
'He's nice,' Maxene said. 'But Snooks! One dry sherry with sufferance.'

The Nightmarkets: a book-length poem-novel set in Melbourne, with a large cast of characters, in nine monologues in various verse-forms. The excerpt here is the opening sequence of the third, 'You Can't Dine Out Forever', spoken by Robert Metcalfe, a young Labor candidate for parliament. An understanding of the events and characters here does not depend on the wider context.

I saw what she meant.
His wife *just* accommodating a white-collar
union official and spouse (Dear's idea).
But polite, so polite.
As we left,
they coyly promised not to divulge we'd actually met.

They're right, I suppose.
I won't tell.   Frank can't stand him: 'He's a bum! Clever,
but a real leper.'   Contact is traitorous.
I nod, knowing, each day
my first thoughts
aren't of the conference or Max or the kids, but *him*,

my opponent, now,
sensibly sleeping.   It's five am. I'm awake
this Saturday in March, ready to drive those
five hundred miles with Frank
(the love-ly!)
Our delegation to the Adelaide national conference.

It's his idea:
'No, no, I'll pay, I'll drive. Let's barbecue for lunch.
We can plan strategies, see the environment —'
His latest hobby is
'plenty of
good fresh air!'   (I fear getting stuck behind semis of sheep.)

But I'm a good boy,
arising on time. Mouth tacky but light-footed,
I succeed not to wake Maxene. And cover
her shoulders, stand staring
Old buddy,
do you really want this: life grafted by chance, work, to mine?

I move to the lounge,
stretch arms over my head, wait. Needn't have bothered.
'Five-thirty,' said the great man. 'Be ready now.'
Six-twenty Max appears.
'Go outside.
He'll blast the horn, wake up Meredith and Daniel —' (she's not cross).

'Go, I'll wait with you.'
Six thirty-three and the late Frank Sutcliffe arrives.
'Sorry,' he beams, 'came across a long lost friend.'
'This hour, this day, a friend?'
'The milko'
(Only you Frank.) I smile, if suffering, though my wife is

infuriated!
She's tutting, blinks into the early morning. *Yes,*
I'll miss you, Maxene. Watched by the paper boy
I look at her, touch and
kiss good-bye.
Frank stands to one side: *whose guardian angel does he think —*

looks skyward, humming,
beams benign as a statesman. Fifteen years older
but onto his, *You're a good boy*, which Maxene hates.
('That Frank, I'll knuckle him!')
Dear buddy,
you'll never buckle to such transparent charm. Just think,

Max, your'e a good girl.
It wouldn't work. He's shrewd enough to slow the act,
and understands you'll never, 'Please bring a plate.'
O'Dowd's own ribdigging
commissar
knows the love-ly Maxene is one of us and looking good.

'See you next week, Max.'
We leave. The news tells us *delegates are heading —*
so between fresh air and '— what's growing on in
the wheat belt —' (err, wheat, Frank),
I've, guess what?
landscapes! horizons! Comrade Sutcliffe! For five hundred miles.

Melton: the news ends,
and he swaps for some beautiful music. I stare,
still waking up round Bacchus Marsh, Frank humming,
blinks behind his horn-rims.
'Wife okay?'
'Quite. And Rita?'   'Looking good, brother. The girl's looking good.'

Myrniong: mmm clck,
his mmm clck. Something worries. I see it licking,
mumbling, clicking. Interested, I ask, Yes?
Wanting him out with it.
Frank pauses.
'They say you're a bit of a ladies man?' And coughs a bit

'Please don't get me wrong.'
And I think of Ye Great They (as mother would say).
Smile seeing him over-reach, almost blushing.
'Only love my wife, not
even you.'
'Even me!' he snorts. 'Not even little me!' (He escapes:

quiet, mumbly, till
Ballan.) 'Bob, it's not that *I* say things, you get me?'
(I do.) 'We can't risk —' (I, once again get him.)
'Now say you're on with, well —
imagine!
And Davison, or a crony, *his* campaign director —'

This scenario
enters Ballarat: our campaign smashed, my name mud.
'They're bums, Bob. It'll be balls for breakfast, Bob.'
It's soap opera, Frank,
the moral
proving your dictum: *lay off the grog, lay off the sheilas.*

I got what he meant?
'Yes Frank they're bums, and prize pricks.'   'You're learning brother.'
(Speaking your language, so I must be, brother.)
Lesson learnt, he diverts
and, so pleased,
recounts my youth, my anti-war anti-conscription past.

(Rather he didn't.)
'Look how they treated you, the bums, the fascist bums.'
I'm certain you mean it but just remember
how, in pre-selection,
you were for
backing Anderson the newsagent, your goat-riding chum.

(Bob's a good, fine lad,
but his past!) Is our trip some getting-to-know-you
act of contrition?   He expands: 'We've our tasks:
You in your small corner —'
Tells me how
'I once served on St George's vestry. Place was full of bums!'

(But he fixed 'em, he
fixed 'em!) 'The love-ly Rita backed me. She's a brick,
a *real* Christian.' And, if not a Christian,
Maxene is a real brick,
a goer:
'— it's all part of doing unto others —'   By Ararat,

we've social justice
and an honest division of profits. At Stawell
he sings, 'I'm get-ting married in th' morn-ing —'
becomes obsessed over
this 'good song'?
Yes, Frank, lovely. And foot down he cruises, de-dumming west.

In the Wimmera,
something is brought to us by Froth Brothers Menswear.
'We have the birthday, but *you* get the presents!'
'How's that, eh?' Frank h'hoos.
'But, y'know,
where would we be without the Froth Brothers of old Aussie?'

And, sentimental
about small business, small businessmen, telling me
'They're one of us', stays expansive. I nod, Yes,
we're a nation of Froths:
all good boys
(other than the bums), giving our presents, the candy kids.

1986

Alex Skovron

b 1948, near Katowice, Poland; arrived in Sydney 1958, moved to Melbourne 1979. He has worked since 1972 as a book editor with various publishers. *The Rearrangement* (1988).

Beyond Nietzsche

'. . . *an infant's littlest, purest love: the kind
born of the moment, not the mind.*'

I

Tonic/dominant, tonic/dominant . . .
One ambulance crushes a thousand ants,
dozing pedestrians pass, or gaping
blunder against each other. A distinguished
father prides himself on self-control, is
irritated, drags his daughter
into a doorway. Tantrum unleashed
he desperately tugs, she lashes out, strikes:
he stuns her with a blow that breaks
his heart for weeks.

Across the road a poet, drunk
in the act of a risky procreation,
pauses. A siren is headed
for a fire, he lifts a shutter
like a half-meant apology, recalls a poem
he never wrote, returns
to his mug of scotch, the corpse
hot to his hand, his aetiology. *The Age
of Reason* hovers half-open by the bed,
her breath is thick.

A list of ants attack
a jamstain on the sink. I drum
the hollow stainless steel to startle them,
they scatter. Finger lightly licked
I pluck the stragglers, flick them in the grass
out the back door. Later
(three a.m.) my baby son squirms
like an insect at my neck.
How easily your children can expose you,
if you listen.

II

Like the stick sun of a small child
every word announces a spindle
of meanings.

An oboe's rim is riddled with minutest creatures;
the calligrapher's sac dispenses
a death-black fluid. Home with child
the heart of Übermensch is bursting
with goodwill: he listens to Requiem K.626
on his gramophone, ponders the meaning
of its dark beauty.
                    Tonic/dominant . . .

Like the rippling pebble of a gazing child
each note unlocks a sun system
of meanings . . .

III

But the ripples will quickly subside,
only the stone will know the weight of the water.
A spiderweb is infinitely trivial:
sitting and patiently waiting,
only the spider . . .

So every meaning conspires against itself
till the littlest love alone can defy meaning,
and every word that makes the world
is half a moon hiding among absent stars.
        Each truth is a half-moon;
        the minutest love alone can escape meaning.

IV

And the galaxies — how swiftly they flick past
on the black train
torpedoing unalterably across the night

in the next suburb . . . It is possible
the shriek that disintegrates a dream means
merely whistle, and a train,
isn't it?

I know a world
where every truth shelters a thousand lies,
each noble thought holds off a swarm of savages
again, and every smile disturbs
a labyrinth of doubts . . . Familiar world.
Sometimes, alone at night
listening for trains, I hear its ghostly dialectic.
        Tonic/dominant, tonic/dominant . . .

And I long for a word free of all its meanings.
        The littlest love.

        [1989]

Schooldream

[from *The Waterline Poems*]

I ran the gauntlet of the years that night,
from first-day kindergartens of an alien food
and brown-smirched toddlers with befuddled legs
through bus-time bullies on the Old South Head
returning from a gruelling primary day
of Englishless encounters by a globe
turned always with the bulging reds in view
for apathetic strangers who could speak.

Then on to nervous corridors of chance
and lizard-tongue retractions from the cane
and useless Wednesday football masquerades
and lessons fraught with mathematic calm . . .
Always before me, like a pair of specs,
the looking-glass horizon steaming up.

        [1990]

Tony Lintermans

b 1948, Melbourne, and lives there; grew up in the country at Lysterfield, south-east of Melbourne. He has worked as a writer of short stories, children's books, TV scripts and political speeches. *The Shed Manifesto* (1989).

The Escape from Youth

My father's discipline closed me like a box.
A hardness hammered shut the lid.
For fifteen years, no matter what he did,
I was unreachable. Venom sealed the locks.

Neutral beauty kept me company. Walking
through neighbours' cattle, from moving skies and trees
I learnt the slower, vaster intimacies.
Avoiding the world of men, I stopped talking,

except intensely to myself. Rumours
of happiness sometimes seeped outside the box.
'Untrue!' I howled, and double-checked the locks.
In the dark, poetry grew like a tumour.

When the poems were big enough to break
their way out, dragging me behind, I saw
my father's face, more bitten than before,
a soft fist eaten by love, impossible to hate.

There is no forgiveness now, nor the need.
Silence bred rich fruits — a known self, those skies —
for which I thank my father. Amnesia lies
behind our peace. Neither of us dares to bleed.

1989

Heat

Under aspens with their white flowers falling
silently as snow, a boy and a girl,
maybe seventeen, leaning through stale air towards
each other, across a table in the packed
Athens square where waiters with silver trays
swerve and swoop, bringing beer, ouzo, mezethes.
I love you, says the boy with believable eyes.

Smooth as pebbles in the sea's mouth, one bleached phrase
among endless collisions of speech, his words
flame towards originality, barrel
through the soft mulch of overuse in centuries

of verse, ballads and popular songs, sliding
between bed sheets rancid with rhetoric
to touch down softly in the pit of her stomach.

Evening with its white locks falling open,
a shady Athens square with its girl and boy
like two cauldrons carrying the same hot liquid
dissolving everything — the square, the tables,
their bodies — into one delicious urgency.
In the evening cool they rise and disappear
down a narrow street where, still burning

they knock at my lit door and find it locked.
Laughing, they walk away quickly, choosing
night with its pale flesh slowly opening.

1989

Alan Gould

b 1949, London, of a British father and an Icelandic mother; arrived in Australia 1966.
Also a writer of fiction, he lives in Canberra. *The Pausing of the Hours* (1984), *Years Found
in Likeness* (1988).

Belfast

The day the store in King William Street burst
the sky rained tailor's dummies, and someone
found an arm three blocks from the blast,
(a fact some papers headlined). When Moran
bumped into his wall of bullets outside
the cartoonshow, amazement not horror
was the crowd's first impulse at such vivid
screenplay. We of course can't take in such nightmare
when the buses still run. 'Unreal' we say, lost
among the flags and statues. On the ghost-
ed Crumlin now, a lone youngster ambles.
She hums a skipping tune as her ball rolls
at the soldier behind the fence, whose each nerve
is a missile triggered on her each move.

1978

Their Finest Hour

At sea, one remembers, time was not an interval
but a flux of dank seasons
of sleep and lookout and sleep,

our seesaw world whitened by the fuggy portholes,
the hull steel slimed with cold sweat.

And as we watched for what big event
might come fizzing at us from the dark,
we noticed the small events below ordinary notice,
how the rare sunlight could pick out
the ocean's sudden candelabra,
how a wave could spread white shawls
of instantaneous lace.

But there is also this eye that watches remembrance,
as though one's entire life
were a flightpath across an epoch.
I note how I descend upon it constantly,
hearing, as I think, the changes of pitch in my descent,
to find there what may have become untrue.

Nonetheless, we have come east of Cape Race
beyond the cover of our aircraft.
The world, which for days
has hurled its white crockery down hatchways,
is clearing to pylons of immense light.
The ocean is minnowed with our merchant ships.
Miles off a corvette is laying depth charge patterns,
raising dazzling tussocks.

And I am moving again in my time of standstill —
who does not have one — childhood or a war?
It centres what will have been my life,
say on a scrambling net
thigh-deep in the black, the quick Atlantic,
handling our boys aboard;
one gleams like coal and vomits engine oil,
one has shut his eyes on grievous burns,
others grin-chatter with the cold.
Poor Devils, I am thinking in a speech
that was once apt, in a time when thought
seemed to have simpler meanings.
I am twenty. I am over sixty.

Time of my standstill
from where the pictures radiate and cool.
Both I and my children
must live in their long light
though differently.

And when my own ship went down, I thought,
If I do not drown,

I will live as a traveller in the peacetime cities,
much as one, emerging from a cinema,
remains enclosed by theatre-dark and the screen's world,
not believing the clamorous traffic
where he frowns on the too-bright street.

But I too was plucked from the black waters
and lived to bellow songs around a piano
in a borrowed suit and my hair slicked
in a vanished style,
                            and live still
in the peace I believed in, but cannot quite believe.

1988

Demolisher

By six he's started. I wake to a wince and arrh,
the animal protests of my neighbour's iron roof.
Behind a cypress-dark, the February sky

is blue as gin. The house is nineteen twenties;
he moves along its apex removing it,
and at this hour he's higher than the sun,

flexing a torso of cinnamon brown, his singlet
dangling whitely from his belt. Slav
or Italian, perhaps, he applies that rigid serpent,

the pinch-bar, to open unconsidered caches
of darkness. His work is wholly restoration —
he is recovering horizons, and

with the long arm of Archimedes, bringing
sunlight to gulf the spiders' vertical suburbs,
dense as hairballs in their sudden light.

So ridge-cap, gutter, sheet iron are grimaced free
from battens; sheets of fibro drop-shatter,
nails, clenched in the pinch-bar's single knuckle,

come out with a sigh. By lunchtime the house
is a birdcage of timbers; by evening it's gone,
and the man sits, gleaming like resin,

rolling cigarettes, drinking water,
looking through a gap at new hills,
peering down the shaft he's made in sixty years.

1988

Edith Speers

b 1949, Canada; arrived in Australia 1974. A biochemist by training, she farms in southern Tasmania. *By Way of a Vessel* (1986).

Australorp

The ships of state
are not so substantial nor sedate
as this black fowl.
Her busty prow ploughs the dusty yard
with all the conceit
of an empire's wealth in her bowels.
No royal matron in mourning has worn
such glittering satin,
such multifrilled crinolines
and patent leather leggings;
nor could she possess so appallingly
the hooked beak
and enamel eyes of respectability.
Barnyard raillery can't dent her disdain.
Her strutting rutting mate
treads upon her back in daylight,
in the public pathway —
she rustles crisp plumage and resumes
a measured pace.
No babes bloody her in their birthing.
She broods moodily over the national assets
and brings forth
in due course
a clutch of incipient self-portraits.
With matriarchal clucking
she instructs them in the ages-old parade:
two steps forward —
scratch, scratch;
two steps back —
peck out a living from the farmyard.

1986

from *Love Sonnets*

Sonnet 9

Darling! I have to see you! Can you come?
Not right now, of course — I'm up to my bum
In boring things I have to do. Why not
Next month? Not Thursday because I work that day;

And what with this and that, all Wednesday's shot;
Tuesdays are so awkward, too. Let's say
A long weekend. But warn me in advance —
It won't be wise to leave it all to chance.

It's such a pity I'm not on the phone,
But call me at my job, that's quite okay,
Otherwise you mightn't find me home —
A shame if you drove down here all that way
For nothing. Which reminds me — I can't cook,
So bring some coleslaw and a barbecued chook.

[1990]

Jennifer Maiden

b 1949, Penrith, west of Sydney, and lives there. She left school at thirteen and did factory work before resuming her education. She has been a teacher of writing for many years, and is also a novelist. *Selected Poems* (1990).

The Mother-in-law
of the Marquis de Sade

To sit people on gas-stove jets,
to plug them into light-sockets,
to prod with sparklers, stand
them barefoot in buckets of dry ice:
              I remember I devised
all these things in the bored
South Africa of childhood,
              the shrill
Brazil that still entrances
the clean children next door
when sometimes as I work
I leave my mind ajar
to overhear their play — unless
their mother hears as well
& threatens them with pain.

        When I was at home
there were jonquils beside the front path
& that word had lonely incision.
        When I was five
all my heroines were 'Jonquil':
now she lingers on, a kind
              of libidinous, sweet
'Shakespeare' but more explicitly

literate & camp. More than most
I always dreamt of princesses & torture,
but dreaded all the fiery
masks of punishment.

I have read that once in the Terror
the Marquis was appointed Magistrate
& none of the felons, not even
his mother-in-law, with whom
he had feuded for life, went to death.
With his books this made his ruin
double in the minds of government.

1978

Space Invaders

Shaun knows you mustn't wait
too long behind the barrier.
You are a target anywhere.
You skip, you strike, you kill
bigger bastards and you score.
He steers his tick-shaped ship across
the black dog universe until
it hits a jet fleet like
a phalanx of fleas and implodes with
the wan beep of a dying
electroencardiograph. He leans
crosslegged in taut boredom,
and hits with sensuous disgust
the infinity of shit he's known
others he's known to need: the stuff
you smoke, the stuff you spend,
the stuff you eat, the stuff
you have to suck at school.
He knows it's not as fucked
as the pokies his parents pull
next door. No handfuls
of shit fall out. His
second ship survives.
He still needs to use his aim,
his hand, his sight.
In spring again he thinks he'll shoot
more wildcats and rabbits with his mate.
He'd like to join the Army soon.
He has a hunter's eye for parasites.

1988

Falling to Prettiness

As children we fell in love
with pictures of clean bedrooms. Pink and green
continental quilts, wallpaper, ferns,
quilted lamps and padded windowseats,
like cells, to make the mouth
water like a womb, mysterious.
The creamy quilts were clouds, the paper
quite drinkable with lavender and doves, all
the lights had dimmers, there were
ashtrays in alabaster, the soft green
of primitive verdure, alcoves
protected velvet books, and prints of meadows
elegant with horses, crocheted women.
The smell of hollyhock and primrose pierced
palpably into the real room, but
who could ever live in such sleek rooms, ever
be able to sip the coyness, with those
rosebuds bright and breakable? We would leave
that windowbox weedy and dry, wet sheets
wrinkled with dawn writhing,
wild sleep.
Tamed rooms are not for nocturnes, not
good places for great long-conversing care.
Well tucked-in somewhere children dream
of neatly waking less than where they are.

1988

The Green Side

Autumn is unquiet everywhere.
Our redhaired Natasha is suing the wind
for sexual harrassment. Somewhere
in South America the C.I.A. is plotting
to overthrow the C.I.A. again. We are
re-elected to the Borstal Board. Yes, there's
no such thing as a bad boy here.
We shot them. All the girls
straddle Yamahas, blush, bush-walk
and come down storming. Natasha
wakes up, her molars grinding
together like rough tiles. In barred air
at her window the leaves dance dying.
Half the tree shakes clumsy crimson.
The green side is still with fear.

1988

Susan Hampton

b 1949, Inverell, north-eastern NSW. She has taught writing and theory courses in Sydney, and now lives in country Victoria. *Costumes* (1982), *Surly Girls* (1989).

Yugoslav Story

Joze was born in the village of Loski Potok,
in a high-cheek-boned family. I noticed
he had no freckles, he liked playing cards,
and his women friends were called Maria, Malcka, Mimi;
and because he was a handsome stranger
I took him for a ride on my Yamaha
along the Great Western Highway
and we ate apples; I'd never met anyone
who ate apples by the case, whose father
had been shot at by Partisans in World War II,
who'd eaten frogs and turnips in the night,
and knew how to make pastry so thin
it covered the table like a soft cloth.
He knew how to kill and cut up a pig
and how to quickstep and polka. He lifted me up in the air.
He taught me to say *'Jaz te ljubim, ugasni luc'*
('I love you, turn off the light')
and how to cook *filana paprika, palacinka,*
and *prazena jetra*. One night in winter
Joze and two of his friends ate 53 *palacinke*
(pancakes) and went straight to the factory
from the last rummy game. Then he was my husband,
he called me *'moja zena'* and sang a dirty song
about Terezinka, a girl who sat on the chimney
waiting for her lover, and got a black bum.
He had four brothers and four sisters,
I had five sisters.
His father was a policeman under King Peter,
my father was a builder in bush towns.
Joze grew vegetables and smoked Marlboros
and he loved me. This was in 1968.

1982

Ode to the Car Radio

My right eye leaking blood coming home
from Casualty, patched, pirate view, & changing gears
past Rooms to Let $12 p.w. beside Surry Hills Smash Repairs
& a beer gut emerging from a pub door at ten, well,
you can picture the general scene

& click! clear as glass, the flute opening
to Prokofiev's *Romeo and Juliet*, cool & sweet
as a parkful of wet trees. Or the time
when a Sutherland aria came blasting through
the stink of rubber at a stop light in Lidcombe,
the volume accidentally on full & I grinned,
mouthing at surprised traffic-jammed faces.
Stopped for a milkshake at the corner of Norton
& Marion Streets, watching clouds coast by
the asbestos-looking steeple of that church —
Pachelbel's *Canon* (I want it played at my funeral)
and the church sailed in towards the city, freed,
the fierce white clouds stayed still.

Diesel fumes from a 470 to Lilyfield spread upward
to Mahler being grandiose, & disappear past a balcony
where an old man (knees spread like a cellist)
reads a newspaper, bowing the strings with scrawny
sun-bitten arms. Oxy-gear lights a Brandenburg Concerto,
car brakes are violins, a jay-walker is moved on
by a French horn. Before too long,
a jack-hammer in Woolloomooloo sounds reasonable
with pizzicato in one ear. The green brush graffitist
writes FRASER IS THE HILTON BOMBER to a Haydn trumpet
& during the downpour after a southerly buster, Debussy
dances on factory rooftops & front lawns &
the whole of Sydney heaves & drifts as the radio
lets out its congruous, incongruous love.

1982

John Forbes

b 1950, Melbourne; educated in New Guinea, Malaya and Sydney. He has lived in Sydney and Melbourne, working intermittently as a furniture removalist, a literary editor and a teacher of writing. *Selected Poems* (1991).

T.V.

dont bother telling me about the programs
describe what your set is like the casing the
curved screen its strip of white stillness like
beach sand at pools where the animals come
down to drink and a native hunter hides his
muscles, poised with a fire sharpened spear

until the sudden whirr of an anthropologist's
hidden camera sends gazelles leaping off in
their delicate slow motion caught on film
despite the impulsive killing of unlucky Doctor
Mathews whose body was found three months later
the film and camera intact save for a faint,
green mould on its hand-made leather casing

1976

Ode/ 'Goodbye Memory'

Goodbye memory & you my distances
calling love me across the vast golf course
to the greens whose flags no wind will ever ruffle
     Goodbye memory & goodbye
to the sheets held against the hot windows
on days when the morning's blue intensity so crushes me
I breathe with the gasps of a fat sprinter & only
a teenybopper's crystal sigh answers, so dumbly,
the immense chances the collision of deckchairs
from the briefcase full of words insomnia unpacks endlessly
     Goodbye memory,
       Goodbye pyjamas
now summer's cool air will rustle forever against my balls
overpowering like a muscle dreams so rusty no art
is bad enough to do their boredom justice
     Goodbye memory
      & the way the mind groans
over its trivia throwing this scrapbook into
the sunrise thinking look how I shine convinced
the day riots because I glance
the mind spoils even the hamburger, training words till
they're all reflex & cooing for torment like a lover
       in love with feeling his love so pure
     So goodbye words
      & goodbye writing, more
ambivalent than a two-brained dinosaur & just as doomed!
      & goodbye to you, poetry
ludicrous sex-aid greasing the statues of my mind
     Hello the yellow beach & the beauty
that closes a book. Hello the suntanned skin
     & underneath that skin, the body.
       Goodbye Memory!

1980

Antipodean Heads

I wish we could be nicer
like the Americans

instead we are caught
half-way between

a European sense of style
you can always be at home in

& the aborigines' knack
of passing the time — they know

that nothing matters too much
between now & forever, unlike

the industrious American
who looks around & sees

that Fate applies her chisel
to his own particular face

so when he stares back at Her
he's warm & essential

not reaching for a quip or a flagon
because he knows these things
are part of what he is

the way a mountain
is carved with the heads
of his Presidents

& we are left to wonder
what shape another 200 years

will leave Ayers Rock in.

1988

Speed, a pastoral

it's fun to take speed
& stay up all night
not writing those reams of poetry
just thinking about is bad for you
                — instead your feelings
follow your career down the drain

& find they like it there
among an anthology of fine ideas, bound together
by a chemical in your blood
that lets you stare the TV in its vacant face
& cheer, consuming yourself like a mortgage
& when Keats comes to dine, or Flaubert,
you can answer their purities
with your own less negative ones — for example
you know Dransfield's line, that once you become a junkie
you'll never want to be anything else?
       well, I think he died too soon,
as if he thought drugs were an old-fashioned teacher
& he was the teacher's pet, who just put up his hand
          & said quietly, 'Sir, sir'
      & heroin let him leave the room.

                1988

Philip Salom

b 1950, Perth; grew up on a dairy farm at Brunswick Junction, WA south-west coast. A graduate in agricultural science, he has had various manual jobs, and teaches writing at Curtin University. *Sky Poems* (1987), *Barbecue of the Primitives* (1989).

Bicentennial — Living Other Lives

At a time when the ruler was troubled by the problems of his subjects, a wise man came to court. He ordered a large bowl filled with water and told the ruler to plunge his head into it. The ruler dreamt of many lives in many places, where justice and riches were plentiful. When he lifted his head from the water, only seconds had elapsed. (Persian tale)

1.

Which lives shall emerge from the waters? Kelly, the armour
turned back into a ploughshare and all his youth unfallowed,
his gift for language and republic
put down deeply, a furrow across the squatters' country.

Burke and Wills, with their shuffling dreams of continent,
survive and tell, their famous buried food rising in gourmet pods
from the desert, so travellers may keep this side of folly
yet know the route of discovery and have the strength to live it.

A murdered woman (the weighed-down backbone of a nation),
who was left behind the humpy or was it the old white Holden —
minute by minute she counts the bullets in her body
as if they were intimate, then flings them down, having done.

Albert Facey and all his kind, children with their backs
worked bare by opportunists, but now the scars from beatings
gone that were a second language, the universal one.
They are its counter-text, rough, naive, unworldly,
this keeps them new and perhaps even more profound.

Soldiers return from the mud, the Last Post just missed,
as always. These men and women, shock-tourists, loved and drunk,
riotous and a bloody insult to the Empire, thank God.
And now awake to that naive willingness to founder for the British.

And all those young lovers, but mostly fathers and mothers —
who died that invisible death on the wrong end of telegrams
burn now those bitter postcards from another country — the strange
handwriting: 'Wish you were here'. (The picture's blank.)

Children rise and breathe again, their skins perfect
and all the sad ways fall from those around them;
the mothers that encircled birth but did not survive it
are themselves born back unto their children.

Aborigines pick out the shot that has sizzled there
like ancestral gravel (a kind they could never guess at).
The boots float back from heads and ribs, bones
find their shape again and the body's country is lived again.

Trugannini and King Billy and their others, come back into the one flesh
from the bare and callous measurers, from the museums'
glass coffins — go back into the place of totem
their white headhunters gone, or utterly uncurious now.

The women are unraped (the man is peeled off like a transfer
or finds every point of contact as he lies over her
burns like a devilish stigmata. She is his electric chair).
Now she can put the pain aside, the horror finally gone.

2.
What will they dream of, under the magic waters
where once they were dead and alert, never letting the self die;
or dead in some spiritual sense of justice, this other self
suffering has laid down like the rings of cambium?

There is no new world. They are refugees, heart-people
from the subtle lands of history. They cannot shock-start
suddenly in a tea-room, the cup nearly at their lips; or in the Ford;
or the next brick laid; a desk of inventions for watering lawns.

Wipe off the water. The impulse of justice is almost
a new colonisation, the latter century under a pith helmet,
or the great body of a leech that must be turned inside-out
to expel its victims. It is the wish for a whole identity.

In each of us there is the exercise of justice.
Without righting anything, there is the gritting tilth of republic
in all these lives. It is the other-body, each life-form intense
and crucial. And all beneath the surface of our words.

All that can be offered is to put them back gently
into death. Where they have felt past rage, indignity,
dishonour. They have all gone, as finally as Holt beneath the waves.
A public peace. Only this second death can give it.

                                                                1987

Bar Sonnet 1

The spirits stand like midgets, each squat chrome bladder
in place, each tiny prick, the slab-backed men all facing in.

Here is the dark-room, windows opaque, the lights snapped on
at opening as the world retreats and the trays swim . . .

Certain words are regular, touch points: the voice going smooth
as leather at each trouser loop. It's home and country wisdom

by these ironists of the public bar: having no use for time
they're stuck with plenty of it. But the talk is tightly buckled,

it holds up, holds in, though heresies have a place in it.
And any speculation, except if it's too clever. Then talk of skill

and the lucky bastard with it, like something big behind the zip
but it's kept pretty level and sounds like somebody else!

It's a language not of heroes, but about them. In silent moments
their eyes move on the barmaid with a kind of pain.

                                                                1987

Properties of the Poet

Fingers and joints for all kinds of tension, also the muscles
of the neck. You've seen these held back until the throat
is like a sleeve packed with wire — they poke into the head-nerve . . .

Shoulders for dejection, joining the above; and joining downwards
to the stomach, this master cylinder of anxieties, which is vaulted
back to the upper chest for ecstasies (everything is so close).

Be leg-long for the various gaits, for leverage on bodies;
the legs — which balance chest or breasts and take you up against . . .
and are wishbone for leading upwards into . . . the apex.

Thigh-skin, the blind-skin of lips and throat for explorations,
the place of the apex itself — the begetting and beguiling sex-parts
for sex, for dreams, for dominations, for balance and abandon.

Thumbs of course for gripping, this human
hand-fang and its double, ghosting in the brain
like a hologram. Sometimes for letting go again.

General skin and skin to wear the touch-prints of things unseen.
Neck-hair, and the small metaphors of the goose
for fear, sudden knowledge, for the hot and chill emotions.

Red and deep voltages and laughter and a heart to shake
(you convulse therefore you am) from anger, loving, irony,
others from the above, from the darkly depressions.

The bottom of the feet — for instincts, the sudden kind
that speak in sweat, and perhaps long-drawn for apprehensions,
for the slow mastery of plodding through the world.

A head for speech, wires for connections and therefore
sometimes for pain, a head for time shifts for the knowing abyss
that sense-storms populate, colloids in the tea-brew of abstractions.

Finally, to the modern surfaces and the primal undercurrents
of the eyes and ears, essential colour jinkers and tone pullers;
these power-holds on attention, and sometimes pretend thinkers.

There's more, but these will do. These and the way they must be held
to know the times, to question the times into intensity.
And maybe come off even. It's not the sort of thing you win.

1989

The Chamber and Chamberlain

The courtroom is underwater opera, aquarium for the deaf.
Counsel and judge flit and pause, mouthing like goldfish,
nuzzling down onto flakes of law, minutiae on the pages
grown like coral. Lines of bubbles stream from the jury —
justice utterly bewilders them, as it should. To compensate,
truth leans twelve different ways, attempts the muscle
of concentration, but who is sure if the jury are swimmers
or singers or part of the set. Justice is the biggest
bubble of the lot. The mumbled points of conceptuality

never prick it: here are the sharks grazing against
the glass. Only the judge remains exotic, his scales
strobing porphyrian above proceedings, or flashing
from the mirth that no-one else is quite permitted,
putting personality where it isn't. The accused stares
with desperate equanimity. She's an example they won't take.

1989

Ania Walwicz

b 1951, Świdnica Śląska, Poland; arrived in Australia 1963, and lives in Melbourne. She
is also a visual artist. *Writing* (1982), *Boat* (1989).

Poland

I forget everything. Now. More and more. It gets dim. And further away. It's
as if I made it up. As though I was never there at all. Not real. Child stories.
Told over and over. Wear thin. This doesn't belong to me anymore. This is
now gone and it left me a long time ago. It doesn't stay with me. This is
the past. This is child. This is too small for me. I grow out of this. I leave
it. I lose my photos. I lost my photos. I only have shreds and bits and pieces.
That come to me now and then. Memory replaces. My shoes get worn. I get
new ones. I can have better time elsewhere. It's all over now. The boat was
here. Now it's moved over the horizon line. When I don't see somebody they
go far away. And they die. I don't keep this. I tried to keep this. I was unhappy
here. To start with. I went back every night. In bed. Think of the station.
Of my town. I can't go back now. It's gone and it's gone. I can't catch it
again. I don't have the smell of it. I don't have the taste of this. I was born
there but I don't remember being born. I wasn't there at all. Not the way
I am now. I never went there. I have nothing to do with this anymore. I could
invent pictures. Slides of a trip. I'm not going to do this. I was very small.
And somebody else. The child is gone now. I was a child once. But I'm not
a child now. It's no good being a child. Somebody always makes you do things.
You are not free to go where you want to go. I leave my child behind. I don't
like it. This is finished and finished. I tell you to go elsewhere. I'm not happy
with this. They ask me where I come from. I say I come from here and here.
This is where I am. Here. I don't remember Poland. I don't want to remember
Poland. I read about it in the papers. And this is not where I am. Not where
I am. I am just here. Now. Poland is a place. On the map. Poland is a name.
I was there once. I was there. But I'm not there now. I'm here. I don't want
to tell stories. I don't want to make things up. I didn't like Poland. I wanted
to travel. I leave my Poland behind. It is gone and it is gone and it is gone.

1982

Little Red Riding Hood

I always had such a good time, good time, good time girl. Each and every day from morning to night. Each and every twenty-four hours I wanted to wake up, wake up. I was so lively, so livewire tense, such a highly pitched little. I was red, so red so red. I was a tomato. I was on the lookout for the wolf. Want some sweeties, mister? I bought a red dress myself. I bought the wolf. Want some sweeties, mister? I bought a red dress for myself. I bought a hood for myself. Get me a hood. I bought a knife.

1982

fairytale

once upon a time there was a king he had three daughters one was very pretty but the two others why they were ugly as hell so he preferred the ugly ones because they were very smart they were very clever indeed he said to them don't worry about getting husbands i mean all right if you want i'll arrange that no problems but you should think about studying first the beautiful one was dumb you see so he didn't like her at all not at all why don't you like me or something she asked him sorry i don't like you because you are stupid so she cried then this fairy heard her and felt sorry for her she better be sent to remedial classes or something the fairy said so she was to help her improve her spelling and stop paying attention to how she looked and all that so all the sisters were all right with the king after that and all getting good marks and scholarships to university because that's very important but the ugly ones started to worry about just how ugly they were so the king arranged for them to have plastic surgery so they looked a lot better after that and were all all right i think but then they wanted to get married after they got their doctorates only after that so that was a problem because they didn't meet many men because they were too busy at their study so the king had to think about what to do because they were driving him crazy all the time talking about getting married and worrying about being old maids so he advertised in the aristocratic gazette for handsome princes to apply so they did but the princesses didn't like them you see they were much too smart for these princes and laughed at them and so forth so that was worrying the king who was getting old by then you see he married late so by that time he was in his eighties and maybe would die he wanted to see the daughters settled so this time he advertised for very clever princes and they came but the princesses found them too ugly and said these men are very good to talk to but as far as looks are concerned forget it wouldn't touch them with a ten foot pole and the thought of kissing them just makes us sick well that was a problem what to do now what was the king supposed to do what were the princesses supposed to do and what were the poor unfortunate rejected princes supposed to do the king suggested maybe you could marry two princes apiece a good looking one for sleeping with and a clever one to talk to but that wasn't such a good idea so the princesses

thought we got to think of something to do after all we got doctorates and
they decided to produce perfect men for themselves the kind that could cook
and be polite and wash·dishes and be willing and able to tell good stories
and the kind that wouldn't annoy them so they set out in the laboratory
to combine all the parts of various princes to make good husbands and they
worked all night but they didn't mind you see they enjoyed their work and
were used to using their heads so lo and behold they made these perfect
husbands by sticking all the pieces of various princes together if one had
good eyes then they took his eyes too bad for him they had to do it and
that was that and some prince would wake up blind too bad they said or
take some prince's legs if they were nice legs they took them they would
take them by special force of their minds and they took them and these men
would wake up sometimes dead but it was all right for the princesses they
didn't mind so they took what they liked and took brains and eyes and legs
and shoulders and took hair and took feet a lot of princes died as a result
and everybody thought that there was a plague and in the end the princesses
had their husbands but they got bored with them and killed them because
they enjoyed working in the laboratory more than marriage

1989

Peter Goldsworthy

b 1951, Minlaton on Yorke Peninsula, SA. He works in Adelaide as a medical practitioner,
and also writes fiction. *Selected Poems* (1991).

Winter Piece

Our son splashes carefully home
from puddle to puddle,
deep stepping stones.

We walk a shout behind
watching from our clothes,
breathing clouds into the sky.

Around us the hard economy of winter,
frugal colour schemes, and underfoot
the worn currency of leaves.

We wrap our coats tighter
sheltering our feelings —
this mundane candle-power of love,

these memories of warmth this morning,
our son between us in the bed,
the coins of rain spilling over the roof.

1982

After Babel

I read once of a valley
where men and women
spoke a different tongue.

I know that any uncooked theory
can find its tribe
— but this might just be true.

For us there are three languages
— yours, mine, and the English between,
a wall of noises.

At times our children interpret,
or music connects our moods.
There are also monosyllables,

the deeper grammar of fucking,
a language too subjective
for nouns.

But even after conjugation
the tense is still the same
— present imperfect.

We take our mouths from each other.
We carry away our tongues,
and the separate dictionaries of our heads.

1982

Suicide on Christmas Eve

After the doctor, the steam-cleaners,
more usefully. I drive home to bed
through intersections sequinned with glass:
it's Christmas Eve, season of donor organs.

What is the meaning of life? I shake you
gently awake. What answer would satisfy?
you mumble, yawning, from Your Side.
To understand is to be bored, you say,
practising, perhaps, for Speech Night.
Knowledge is a kind of exhaustion, you say.

A child enters our room: is it morning yet?
Not Yet. In another room the lights of the Tree
wink colourfully, and when the telephone rings
again, it is almost, but not quite, in time.

1988

John Foulcher

b 1952, Sydney. He teaches in a secondary school, and lives at Maianbar, south of Sydney. *Pictures from the War* (1987), *The Black Paperweight* (1991).

Innes Foulcher (1897-1984)

The lace curtains in their living room
were like barbed wire, keeping the carpets from fading;
the furniture was sullied with a mineshaft light.

Everywhere, there were pictures of stiff-collared men
and crushed white women in bonnets,
cowled about the piano.

Nellie, her sister, lived by the piano
and died by it, never knowing the unstarched hearts of men,
fearing them, perhaps:

she would cycle in wool-heavy heat
with her skirt clinging to her calves, the clipped spinnakers of cloth
billowing, like a storm.

I can't recall colours there, in that Christian house.
But Innes took Christ and all the ranting prophets
out of this, led them

through the Pacific's wilderness
to Fiji, where she lived thirty years,
scalded with sun and work.

Some photos I've seen: Innes among the natives,
like a pillar of salt
or a sharp vein of quartz through their onyx bodies,

splendidly missed
when she returned for Eric, the mongoloid brother
Nellie couldn't cope with, alone.

I remember the early Christmases,
our visits after church, and Eric
with his grub-bellied tongue and lizard eyes.

We saw them always together: Nellie and Innes,
grey puffs of hair, and hands chattering with teacups,
words that hovered in the room

like blowflies.
How like coming out from underground it was,
running to the gate and the car beyond.

Innes out-lived them both,
moved to Bowden Brae, the retirement village,
with its coal-mine corridors and ceilings,

its assumption that age diminishes.
It was 'modern', but she filled it with her old house,
chipped floral crockery

on the vinyl tabletop.
From the window, the road stuttered between trees,
and the wind chanted

among the iron verandah rails;
ingots of sunlight were stacked by the bed
when, finally, she died, the last of the Foulcher girls.

How little we knew of her.
At the funeral, a vague succession of Foulchers
lined the front pews,

like milk bottles in a crate, each having a name
from somewhere in the Christmas conversations
of that dark house;

but, after the last prayers, five Fijians stood
and sang for her, all the island's flowers
opening, in their voices.

1987

Marriage

I passed my last exam in 1975, and left university
as a refugee flees a ruined city.

The war in Vietnam had finished. There was
that frantic, out-of-focus guerilla
pounding up the steps of the U.S. embassy;
and the helicopters, silent and dark, drifting away from Saigon.

In that January, we were married. The wedding
snapped us from the past
like twigs. Broke,

we went north for a week, and made love every day.
At Avoca, we stood at the cliff's edge,
the sea oiled with dusk;

stood there, above waves that slumped on the dull brown rocks
as a congregation kneels to pray —
mosquitoes were scattered about like confetti.

Coming back to Sydney,
we had nothing, and nowhere to go,
so we slept on my mother's loungeroom floor. The next morning,
waking, I heard my mother

rattling cups in the kitchen; and the radio, with its news
of cruelty, and poverty, and war.

1987

Myron Lysenko

b 1952, Heyfield, eastern Victoria, of Ukrainian parents. He has worked as a labourer
and as a clerk in Melbourne, and teaches writing. *Coughing with Confidence* (1988).

Living in Coburg

I'm a silly boy. A lazy city boy,
sitting in my house drinking beer
& reading newspapers,
surrounded by Italian neighbours
who don't understand
my weeds & run-down house.
They believe in food & neatness
& photography & families.
They stand in front of their homes
posing for cameras & relatives,
making sure they don't block out
the manicured lawns
& the colours of the stylish flowers
or the new car, washed & gleaming
in the pebbled concrete drive-way.
They mail their homes to Italy.

They're nice to me; they wave & smile
when I walk past their lives.
They talk to each other about my house —
want to buy it for their daughters.
They don't complain about my stereo,
don't ask about the strange looking friends
popping in & out of my doors
or too much about my life-style.
They wonder why I'm too weak
to push the lawn mower around.
They meander past my house
when they go visiting in the street,
wondering what I'm doing *in here*

with my loud music & closed blinds.
They would like to see more of me
in the front yard.

They tempt me with their food smells
& the way they laugh & talk
when they get excited.
They knock on my door & ask
if they can cut down the trees
which are tearing up their drive-ways
& pulling down their fences;
& while they're at it
could they possibly mow my lawns
or at least the front one, please?
& maybe next week they could plant flowers
because flowers make a house look good;
& if I'd like, they could turn my back yard
into a huge vegetable garden,
altho, of course, they'd leave enough room
for me to sunbake.

They carry a bottle of beer up my drive
& they bring their own glasses
& they talk about football & unemployment
& their children, studying at uni.
They ask how long I intend to live here
on my own, surrounded by families.
They tell me not to sell the house
without talking to them first
& they say goodbye & smile
as they carry the empty bottle down my drive
sweeping the dirt off my path
with their coloured rubber gumboots;
& over the kitchen table they tell their families
that I'm thinking of moving to another suburb
to be with people my own age
& they look out their windows
at me, in the back yard, lying in the sun,
dreaming about going to Italy.

1988

Chris Mansell

b 1953, Sydney. She is a literary editor, teaches writing at the University of Wollongong, and lives at Berry, NSW south coast. *Head, Heart, Stone* (1982), *Redshift/Blueshift* (1988).

Definition Poem: Pissed as a Parrot

For those of you who are etymologically inclined
I would like to take this opportunity
to explain to you the derivation of the expression
pissed as a parrot.

Sidney Baker in *The Australian Language* indexes
     Paroo dog
     Parrot
     Parson's pox
There is no entry under *pissed.*
He also gives
     Proverbial, come the
     Piss, panther's
and   Pseudoxy.

Parrot on page 55 is a sheep
which has lost some of its wool.
If the sheep's fly-blown it's a rosella.

Wilkes in his *Australian Dictionary of Colloquialisms*
lists only to piss in someone's pocket
(refer Kylie Tennant, Bray, Hardy & Herbert)
Pissant around (Dymphna Cusack)
and Pissant, game as a.
There is no mention of any parrot in any condition at all.

In *Collins English Dictionary* (Australian edition)
you will find definitions for
     piss
     piss about
     Pissaro
     piss artist
and   piss off.

Parrots appear in their psittaciformes capacity
which I found meant having a short hooked bill,
compact body, bright plumage, and an ability
to mimic.
It was not entirely clear whether this referred to birds.

Parrot-fashion had nothing to do with anything.

Roget's *Thesaurus*
Nuttal's *Dictionary of Synonyms and Antonyms*
Stillman's *Poet's Manual and Rhyming Dictionary*
Webster's *Treasury of Synonyms, Antonyms and Homonyms*
and the *Shorter Oxford English Dictionary*
were no help at all.

I thought *Usage & Abusage*
being by Partridge
could be illuminating, but it appears
that neither piss nor parrots are abused.

I refused to consult Strunk's *Elements of Style*
on the grounds that the backcover blurb
has quotes from the *Greensboro Daily News*
and *The Telephone Engineers and Management Journal.*

But I went to afternoon tea
in the School of Chemistry at the University of Sydney
at 4 pm on Thursday 6 November
and there, Dr A.R. Lacey, physical chemist, MSc PhD,
informed me, in his capacity as a true blue,
down to earth, dinky-di, grass roots Aussie that
when working on his horse stud in the Wingecarribee Shire
he had observed that Gang Gang cockatoos
fall with paralytic suddenness
from the branches of Hawthorn bushes
after ingesting the berries.

Incredibly, *The Reader's Digest Complete Book of Australian Birds*
makes no mention of this.

1982

Overtime

I resigned
three months ago
(the job
not myself)

Now
I dream about it sweat
there's a corridor
someone yells *bark*
I bark
I bark down the corridor
bark

someone yells *bark*
again
and I bark
down the corridor
bark
down the corridor
I *bark*.
It goes on like this
til morning.

The next night
the corridor
I recognise.
No one there.
I yell *bark*
all night.

Bark I yell
bark
they don't come into
the yellow corridor
but I *bark*
anyway.

Tomorrow
I have an interview
for a different job.
I want the money
not it.
I'm almost certain
there'll be
another corridor there.

1988

Philip Mead

b 1953, Brisbane; educated in Australia, England and USA. He teaches writing and Australian literature at the University of Melbourne. *This River Is in the South* (1984).

The Man and the Tree

for David Campbell

I felt the season changing in the yard today
along the wooden fence and in the leaves.
The almond is always first to break in flower
and everything it has it gives.

There was a man standing underneath in innocence,
    whose place was there, whose face
    was hurt with years like the branches.
    He was saying what the tree was saying:
    this is your sign of mutability and joy.

Make your speech from what is living, here.
    Work to know the word that's damp
    underneath like a stone, the word
    that harvests in the sun, the half-word
    she turns in her sleep to say.

Make your sentence lead the life you lead,
    and when it comes, there will be art
    to choose the simplest word of all.

The almond tree in Spring is brave,
    all it says is honour life
    and take the new growth as chance.
Look how the passion in the moving of the season
    loosens conversation in the heart.
Be with us as a bearing tree, in flower,
    growing in the world, now that
    all you made has let the winter in.

1984

Words which may be confounded, or Dewdrops from the Manse

There's all this dreck floating around in our minds,
or at least in mine there is   old addresses, telephone numbers,
hundreds of bits of old and new songs from *I Pagliacci* to Green Grow the
    Rushes O,
lists of children's names, jacks-in-the-box of horror and misadventure
that keep jumping out as boars' heads couped at the neck or yellow-eyed
greyhounds, especially during insomnia and won't be battened down,
lots of steamy cartoon fantasies beginning 'O Veronica, let's throw
away the past; we need each other now!' or 'I was a rich man's play-thing...'
or remembered sections from old grammar books   Ambiguous Sentences
Shades of Meaning   American Demons   and proverbs I've never really
had a chance to put into circulation like Words without deeds are rushes
and reeds or friendly, fairly useless words like incunabula, revanchist
or nugatory (who doesn't think of confectionery first?) and packed away
with the smell of mosquito coils and mustard pickles and the sound
of a mantel-clock being wound, hundreds of other Proustian dead-letters
waiting for their small untimely deliveries — some will wait forever.

Imperfectly remembered details of Baron Corvo's time in Venice,
or the 'Battered Ornaments' entry in Fowler's, the Mister Whippy van,
the names of old teachers, some of the colour words from a childhood
watercolour set, embarrassing moments from adolescence, advertising jingles,
epigrams, scout troop totem names, Phillip, Hunter, King, Bligh, Macquarie
Mary Jo Kopechne, fragments of remembered illustrations like the Ishtar Gate,
sinisterly striped radar dishes, ashtrays made from miniature Goodyear
tyres, steel ammunition boxes in the back yard used as fish tanks,
old-fashioned wooden toys that we remember almost with tears, french-
        knitting
reels, bits of dried bladder-wrack, stills from *Dersu Uzala* or
The Trouble With Harry, odd occult symbols and tables of weights and
        measures,
alpha-beta-gamma, aleph-beth-gimel, Phantom rough on roughnecks (old jungle
saying) . . . and all this is only for the nonce too! Any other moment
is another whole heap of different litter. And as if that weren't enough
there's that crazy witzarbeit running amuck through all this like
The Dance of the Hours looking for possibilities   isn't Fern Fronds
and Wattle Whispers a nice title?   or how about The Waist Land
Rubbery Underarms, Pelf-Portrait in a Convict's Mirror, The Terrible
Parable of Clarabelle the Unbearable? And then in the midst of these
hundreds of thousands of megabits of random junk with no purpose
but the idle copia of self-filler — but this isn't *me*! — there seems to come
a creaturely voice which may be ours, with the sound of good tidings
saying   It's lovely here   but in fact it is saying something much older
and harsher only we've just started to hear it, somewhere deeply inside
where it is still and more than a little appalled   Deliver us from
the blank and the dark   Save us from what will happen anyway
Heard again through the debris of place-names — Luxor, Maroochydore,
        Bungendore
Tübingen, hippie-kitsch silver ankhs, metal fourex trays, sobranie cocktails,
cloches, svelte grey hombergs and hundreds of treasured family snapshots,
the memory of slanting-sunlight through bamboo brakes
as though it were, I don't know, Rilke, somehow mixed up in all this,
deeply tender, bending close to our ear, *lento* now   Art is never kind.
Life is always unfinished   And so on and on, and wider and wider,
infinitely, boringly, like some harmless but strangely disconcerting
topiary garden, stretching off towards a distant horizon
but without any kind of closed effect. Taking up all this space, flooding
        through time.

                                                        [1986]

Kevin Hart

b 1954, London; arrived in Australia aged ten; grew up in Brisbane. He teaches literary studies at Deakin University in Geelong. *Your Shadow* (1984), *Peniel* (1990).

A History of the Future

There will be cities and mountains
as there are now,

and steeled armies
marching through abandoned Squares
as they have always done.

There will be fields to plough,
the wind will shake the trees, acorns
will fall,

and plates will still crack
for no apparent reason.

And that is all we can truly know.

The future is over the horizon, we cannot hear
a word its people say,

and even if they shout to us
to make us cease
bombing their lands, destroying their cities,

a shout from there would sound like an acorn
dropped on cement,

or a plate on the shelf
beginning to crack.

1981

Flies

I could never get rid of you
no matter what the room or street:
at meals, kissing my first girl, walking by the river,
you joined me
and now you bring it back to me.

Flies: an imitation of 'Las moscas' by Antonio Machado (1875-1939).

I don't know what minute books you read
upon my ceiling —
the prayers of fallen angels, perhaps —
you sing the song
the radio plays between its channels.

On summer afternoons
when the sun has halved the day's allowance of air,
you dart around
like tadpoles in the coolest water
and make me feel as heavy as my bed.

I've watched your dated soft-shoe act
on blackboards, nuns, and men with picks;
and when, inflamed with Marx,
I gave up God,
you sang of the equality of flies.

But I know
that you have rested on my oldest toys,
upon my Latin grammar,
my love-letters, and my Grandfather's dying face.
I know you live off filth, I know

you never work like bees
and certainly never shine like butterflies;
and yet, old friends,
this morning as I hear your buzz
you bring my past all back to me, like honey and light.

1984

The Last Day

When the last day comes
a ploughman in Europe will look over his shoulder
and see the hard furrows of earth
finally behind him, he will watch his shadow
run back into his spine.

It will be morning
for the first time, and the long night
will be seen for what it is,
a black flag trembling in the sunlight.
On the last day

our stories will be rewritten
each from the end,
and each will end the same;

you will hear the fields and rivers clap
and under the trees

old bones
will cover themselves with flesh;
spears, bullets, will pluck themselves
from wounds already healed,
women will clasp their sons as men

and men will look
into their palms and find them empty;
there will be time
for us to say the right things at last,
to look into our enemy's face

and see ourselves,
forgiven now, before the books flower in flames,
the mirrors return our faces,
and everything is stripped from us,
even our names.

1984

Judith Beveridge

b 1956, London; arrived in Australia 1960, lives in Sydney. Her occupations have included library assistant and teacher of writing. *The Domesticity of Giraffes* (1987).

Catching Webs

A fragrance would call me out of the house:
threads sweet with pollens.

I'd walk into any alien zone or quiet radar —
(those stolen threads always fitted so close).
And sometimes coming back into the house
I'd feel a thread break across my lips.

I remember the white purdah of those days
spent amongst the undergarments of trees,
air crisp as dressmaker's paper
against the bright textile of summer.

I was a child with so much of my world
snatched up in a mending, as life unspooled
from my fingers though I could not feel
those long strands trailing to the South.

I'd go out after meals to watch a thread
trace itself on the sky and wait for it
to drift into my hands; or walk amongst
the flowers draped in the negligee

of their leaves. I remember sky
on rising sky, cool air on my lips,
stars that sewed themselves onto the air
like buttons in order of brightness

and a child's heart pushing in
like a needle, making a pattern
of its incisions; making a web
out of the stitch of its own silence:

thin thin darning that holds the heart separate
from its white dress. I knew a thread
could be pulled right through
the human body. In the fragrant air,

I felt the moon in my blood, trailing its wedding.

1987

The Domesticity of Giraffes

She languorously swings her tongue
like a black leather strap as she chews
and endlessly licks the wire for salt
blown in from the harbour.
Bruised-apple eyed she ruminates
towards the tall buildings
she mistakes for a herd:
her gaze has the loneliness of smoke.

I think of her graceful on her plain —
one long-legged mile after another.
I see her head framed in a leafy bonnet
or balloon-bobbing in trees.
Her hide's a paved garden of orange
against wild bush. In the distance, running
she could be a big slim bird just before flight.

Here, a wire-cripple —
legs stark as telegraph poles
miles from anywhere.
She circles the pen, licks the wire,
mimics a gum-chewing audience

in the stained underwear of her hide.
This shy Miss Marigold rolls out her tongue

like the neck of a dying bird.
I offer her the fresh salt of my hand
and her tongue rolls over it
in sensual agony, as it must
over the wire, hour after bitter hour.
Now, the bull indolently
lets down his penis like a pink gladiolus
drenching the concrete.

She thrusts her tongue under his rich stream
to get moisture for her thousandth chew.

1987

Gig Ryan

b 1956, Melbourne; moved to Sydney 1978. She has worked in various clerical jobs and is also a songwriter and performer in a band, Disband. *Manners of an Astronaut* (1984), *Excavation* (1990).

If I Had a Gun

I'd shoot the man who pulled up slowly in his hot car this morning
I'd shoot the man who whistled from his balcony
I'd shoot the man with things dangling over his creepy chest
in the park when I was contemplating the universe
I'd shoot the man who can't look me in the eye
who stares at my boobs when we're talking
who rips me off in the milk-bar and smiles his wet purple smile
who comments on my clothes. I'm not a fucking painting
that needs to be told what it looks like.
who tells me where to put my hands, who wrenches me into position
like a meccano-set, who drags you round like a war
I'd shoot the man who couldn't live without me
I'd shoot the man who thinks it's his turn to be pretty
flashing his skin passively like something I've got
to step into, the man who says *John's a chemistry Phd*
and an ace cricketer, Jane's got rotten legs
who thinks I'm wearing perfume for him
who says *Baby you can really drive* like it's so complicated,
male, his fucking highway, who says *ah but you're like that*
and pats you on the head, who kisses you at the party because
everybody does it, who shoves it up like a nail

I'd shoot the man who can't look after himself
who comes to me for wisdom
who's witty with his mates about heavy things
that wouldn't interest you, who keeps a little time
to be human and tells me, female, his ridiculous
private thoughts. Who sits up in his moderate bed
and says *Was that good* like a menu
who hangs onto you sloppy and thick as a carpet
I'd shoot the man last night who said *Smile honey*
don't look so glum with money swearing from his jacket
and a 3-course meal he prods lazily
who tells me his problems: his girlfriend, his mother,
his wife, his daughter, his sister, his lover
because women will listen to that sort of rubbish
Women are full of compassion and have soft soggy hearts
you can throw up in and no-one'll notice
and they won't complain. I'd shoot the man
who thinks he can look like an excavation-site
but you can't, who thinks what you look like's for him
to appraise, to sit back, to talk his intelligent way.
I've got eyes in my fucking head. Who thinks if he's smart
he'll get it in. I'd shoot the man who said
Andrew's dedicated and works hard, Julia's ruthlessly ambitious
who says *I'll introduce you to the ones who know*
with their inert alcoholic eyes
that'll get by, sad, savage, and civilised
who say *you can* like there's a law against it
I'd shoot the man who goes stupid
in his puny abstract how-could-I-refuse-she-needed-me
taking her tatty head in his neutral arms like a pope
I'd shoot the man who pulled up at the lights
who rolled his face articulate as an asylum
and revved the engine, who says *you're paranoid*
with his educated born-to-it calm
who's standing there wasted as a rifle
and explains the world to me. I'd shoot the man who says
Relax honey come and kiss my valium-mouth blue.

1980

So What

Separate things are coming at you.
From the front room, cute jazz. Is it?
This slop hovering in the background like a new Hawaii,
and here, for instance, you're communicating things,
but in my head a last hour finds sense
and it becomes what I say it is.
Like his sadness makes you sad. Dumb to feel,
to wonder. If the night wasn't black, would you
with your turning heart, ever listen? Are you?
My dear invention, you can go now.
I've got this much, and your stunned key works.
His brain's small seeds pass for bright.
And downstairs still, music circulates.
I wish the night outside would come in.
Unload the door.
The sufferer may be crowned
but can you sleep like that, your eyes
jutting from door to stair to window,
waiting for that wrist of light to jam or just come home.

1984

Two Winters

[from *Three Poems*]

I learn at the museum Van Gogh is never cold
The young painters talk a lot
At home he's stoned in glory
The grand lines of the shopping arcades warm and lose me
He deals out the photos like cards
I walk beneath the wriggling towering statues
the silky skating water's shattered pews of orange light
letters dating and rusting
His lying singing voice warbles but nothing hurts me
Advertising welcomes the cold travellers

I remember his black sweat hair and lava
and hammering in his head like mud
The buildings slant in the canal
silk mirrors craven and broke
Without him I feel empty and alive
the happy eighteenth century clocks the desk skulls

[1990]

Robert Walker

1958–84; b Port Augusta, SA, into an Aboriginal family of fifteen; grew up in country areas of SA and in Adelaide. He died after a violent encounter with prison officers in Fremantle, WA. *Up, Not Down, Mate!* (1981).

Life Is Life

The rose among thorns
may not feel the sun's kiss each mornin'
and though it is forced to steal the sunshine
stored in the branches by those who cast shadows,
it is a rose and it lives.

1981

Solitary Confinement

Have you ever been ordered to strip
Before half a dozen barking eyes,
Forcing you against a wall —
Ordering you to part your legs and bend over?

Have you ever had a door slammed
Locking you out of the world,
Propelling you into timeless space —
To the emptiness of silence?

Have you ever laid on a wooden bed —
In regulation pyjamas,
And tried to get a bucket to talk —
In all seriousness?

Have you ever begged for blankets
From an eye staring through a hole in the door,
Rubbing at the cold air digging into your flesh —
Biting down on your bottom lip, while mouthing 'Please, Sir'?

Have you ever heard screams in the middle of the night,
Or the sobbings of a stir-crazy prisoner,
Echo over and over again in the darkness —
Threatening to draw you into its madness?

Have you ever rolled up into a human ball
And prayed for sleep to come?
Have you ever laid awake for hours
Waiting for morning to mark yet another day of being alone?

If you've never experienced even one of these,
Then bow your head and thank God.
For it's a strange thing indeed —
This rehabilitation system!

1981

Philip Hodgins

b 1959, Shepparton, north-central Victoria, where he grew up on a dairy farm. He lived in Melbourne, before moving to the state's central-west in 1990. Since 1983 he has been undergoing treatment for leukaemia. *Blood and Bone* (1986), *Animal Warmth* (1990).

Making Hay

In rectangular vertigo the balepress
gives prodigious birth.
From conception to delivery
takes less than a minute.
Humming down slow rows
of lucerne and paspalum it chews grass,
snakeskins, thistles, feathers, anything.
By midday it can do no more.
The paddock is a maze of compression
soon to be unravelled
by hay-carters starting at the edges.
Shirtless in cowskin chaps and gloves
they perform their complex dance
with eighty-pound bales
on an earthquaking load that shoves
a slackchained,
bouncing, banging, balesucking escalator
down bays of the marvellous smell
of cut grass.
When the dance is done,
easing to the monolith, they sit
with cigarettes on what they've made.
After the hay has been restacked
they take a big tyre tube
to the swimming hole and muddy the water
worse than cattle,
slushing after the slippery tube.
With one stye eye and sleek
black skin it is the nearest thing
to a leviathan in this billabong.

1986

Ich Bin Allein

'Cancer is a rare and still scandalous subject for poetry;
and it seems unimaginable to aestheticize the disease.'
Susan Sontag, *Illness as Metaphor*

It is in every part. Nothing can be cut off or out.
A steady suddenness.
It isn't Keats
or randomness.
It is this body
nurturing its own determined death.
I will find out how much pain is in this body
and I will not behave myself.
It isn't fit for poetry
but since
poets create their own mythology
there is no choice.
My friends have all gone home.
I'm in the dank half-light. I am alone.

1986

The Pier

Upset about death you go for a walk
and finish up down at the pier
watching the old men with their long rods

that doodle slowly like distraction.
It's overcast and out there on the bay
squalls are circling like seagulls.

The pier runs a hundred metres into the sea
and you notice that the beams
of oregon or whatever across the top of it

are weathered as blunt at their ends
as the fingers of those fishermen
and that the big wooden thumbs

where a ship would be tied up
are neatly capped with bird-droppings.
Each time a wave crashes along underneath

there is the rickety sound of train travel
and the two rows of tree trunks
supporting and extending the platform

are worn away a little bit more.
Above the waterline they look complete
but when that line breathes down

it's worrying to see how much
the lower parts have been decayed away
and you imagine it all collapsing in the future.

The further out you go the more
those trunks have been weakened
in the place they most need to be secure

and the deeper the water looks
(so deep it's hard to figure out
just how they would have built the pier)

until on a plank made slippery
with scales and fishgut stains and seaspray
you come to the end.

[1990]

Alison Croggon

b 1962, Carltonville, Transvaal, South Africa; moved to England 1966, and to Australia 1969, where she grew up near Ballarat, Victoria. She is a freelance journalist and drama critic in Melbourne. *This Is the Stone* (1991).

Domestic Art

[from *Quickening*]

1. Labour

pain grabbed me cruelly and tossed me
into the violent land of my body.
all around were ravines and crags
and the freefall of exhaustion.
the only way out was through. at the end
you split out of me like a ripe seed
and opened your unused eyes on my sweating skin.

2. Hymn

neither maid nor matchless
neither still nor blest
I woke with knowledge in my womb
and fear within my breast

the day was five hours old
when Joshua wriggled out
to check what all the dim reports
of noise were all about

he is a knot of needs
my ends are all astray
but the hours are short and fat
with Joshua in my day

3. Cooking

rise into me like new cake
bunched and sorry you loud snout
bursting your sheaf of blind
legs you list of fists writing
all over me squiggles and
drizzles of must o my
juicy suckling out of the
oven and perfectly
crusted all over with smiles

4. Washing

There's nothing much surprising about washing nappies
except that shit is such strange colours, a sloppy spectrum of yellow.
You become inured to it, like standing in cowpats for warmth
on frost mornings or mucking out stables with your hands.
However, it's no accident that Jesus
washed the feet of his disciples.
Folding the laundered cloths, you may find
an unsettling capacity for grace.

5. Baby

I am a ball of thumbs
eyeing the suckable world

it's full of winks and smiles
and colours like food

my innards snarl and yap
I shall not sleep

in case I wake alone
in the skinless dark

6. Passional

you open and shut like wavelidded oceans you squall your greed you
    offer your treasures
humbly I unravel your absolute languages

you sprang from love like a new god unstable and charged as weather
a tyrant of toilsome needs I bend low and serve you
now I feel my funeral its alleluias
arching under my flat pulse
holding your hard skull a helpless worship utterly dependent utterly
    separate

always under the patches and scuffs the indomitable cell the living
    pattern of you

my soul is elastic my senses billow like nets to draw in your voices
your sleep lipping my sleep my sunflower skin beaming to you
more than the shock of reflection rather a blaze
in a mansion of unknown rooms and my chilled
hunger welcomed in and generously feasted at a table always my own

7. Domestic Art

somewhere a poem is invented
    for a sleeping child it has
a greek simplicity the whitest
    sheets to signify
the unwritten the poem
may contain a flute or a slow
    drum but no
sharp instruments even tho
the crescents pencilled in
by sleep and the breath are
    easily erasable the poem
bruises secretly the deepest
    muscles of pleasure

1990

Acknowledgements

For permission to reprint copyright material in this collection, grateful acknowledgement is made to the copyright holders, as follows:

ROBERT ADAMSON: The author for 'Dead Horse Bay' from *Selected Poems* (Angus & Robertson, 1977), 'Into Forest' from *The Law at Heart's Desire* (Prism Books, 1982) and 'Dreaming Up Mother' from *The Clean Dark* (Paper Bark Press, 1988). BRUCE BEAVER: Collins/Angus & Robertson Publishers for poem X from 'Letters to Live Poets', from *Selected Poems* (1979); University of Queensland Press for 'Machine' from *Charmed Lives* (1988). JUDITH BEVERIDGE: Black Lightning Press and the author for 'Catching Webs' and 'The Domesticity of Giraffes' from *The Domesticity of Giraffes* (1987). JOHN BLIGHT: Collins/Angus & Robertson Publishers for 'The Spit' and 'Bee's Sting' from *Selected Poems 1939-75* (1976). VINCENT BUCKLEY: Collins/Angus & Robertson Publishers and The Estate of Vincent Buckley for 'No New Thing', sections VII-X from 'Golden Builders' and 'Origins' from *Selected Poems* (1981). CAROLINE CADDY: Fremantle Arts Centre Press for 'Letters from the North' from *Letters from the North* (1985). DAVID CAMPBELL: Collins/Angus & Robertson Publishers and Judith Campbell for 'The Australian Dream', 'Snake', 'Crab' and 'August' from *Collected Poems* (1989), and 'Clarinets' from *The Man in the Honeysuckle* (1979). HAL COLEBATCH: Collins/Angus & Robertson Publishers for 'Third Song of Popeye the Sailorman' and 'Visiting Dachau, 1973' from *Outer Charting* (1985). ALISON CROGGON: The author for 'Domestic Art'. JACK DAVIS: The author and Houghton Mifflin Australia for 'Camped in the Bush' from *The First-born and Other Poems* (Angus & Robertson, 1970; J.M. Dent Pty Ltd, 1983) and 'John Pat' from *John Pat and Other Poems* (Houghton Mifflin Australia, 1988). BRUCE DAWE: Longman Cheshire for 'The Not-so-good Earth', 'The Raped Girl's Father', 'Homecoming', 'Planning a Service', 'The Sadness of Madonnas' and 'An Epiphany' from *Sometimes Gladness* (1988). ROSEMARY DOBSON: Collins/Angus Robertson Publishers for 'Autobiography', 'The Spring of Naupaktos' and 'Canberra Morning' from *Selected Poems* (1980); Hale & Iremonger Pty Limited for 'The Nightmare' from *The Three Fates & Other Poems* (1984). MICHAEL DRANSFIELD: University of Queensland Press for 'Fix' and 'A Strange Bird' from *Collected Poems* (1987). GEOFFREY DUTTON: The author for 'Comfort' from *A Body of Words* (Edwards and Shaw, 1977) and 'Love and Complacency' from *Selective Affinities* (Angus & Robertson, 1985). ANNE ELDER: Mr John Elder for 'The Love Fight' and 'The Two Sides' from *For the Record* (Hawthorn Press, 1972). DIANE FAHEY: Dangaroo Press for 'Eileithyia' from *Metamorphoses* (1988); the author for 'Remembering Ophelia' and 'Dressmaker' from *Turning the Hourglass* (Dangaroo Press, 1990). JOHN FORBES: The author for 'T.V.' from *Tropical Skiing* (Angus & Robertson, 1976) and 'Ode/"Goodbye Memory"' from *Stalin's Holidays* (Transit Poetry, 1980); Hale & Iremonger Pty Limited for 'Antipodean Heads' and 'Speed, a pastoral' from *The Stunned Mullet* (1988). JOHN FOULCHER: Collins/Angus & Robertson Publishers for 'Innes Foulcher (1897-1984)' and 'Marriage' from *Pictures from the War* (1987). KEVIN GILBERT: The author for '"Consultation"' from *People Are Legends* (University of Queensland Press, 1978); Penguin Books Australia Ltd for 'Mum' from *Inside Black Australia* (1988). BARBARA GILES: Pariah Press and the author for 'Learning All the Words in the World' from *Earth and Solitude* (1984), and for 'Fireworks and Champagne' and 'Almost out of Breath' from *The Hag in the Mirror*

(1989). PETER GOLDSWORTHY: The author for 'Winter Piece' and 'After Babel' from *Readings from Ecclesiastes* (Angus & Robertson, 1982), and for 'Suicide on Christmas Eve' from *This Goes with This* (ABC Enterprises, 1988). ALAN GOULD: University of Queensland Press for 'Belfast' from *Icelandic Solitaries* (1978); Collins/Angus & Robertson Publishers for 'Their Finest Hour' and 'Demolisher' from *Years Found in Likeness* (1988). ROBERT GRAY: Collins/Angus & Robertson Publishers for 'The Meatworks', 'Late Ferry', 'Bondi' and 'The Lake' from *Selected Poems* (1990). SUSAN HAMPTON: The author for 'Yugoslav Story' and 'Ode to the Car Radio' from *Costumes* (Transit Poetry, 1982). J. S. HARRY: Island Press for 'a shot of war' and 'wind painting' from *A Dandelion for Van Gogh* (1985). KEVIN HART: Golvan Arts Management Pty Ltd and the author for 'A History of the Future' from *The Lines of the Hand* (Angus & Robertson, 1981), and for 'Flies' and 'The Last Day' from *Your Shadow* (Angus & Robertson, 1984). GWEN HARWOOD: Collins/Angus & Robertson Publishers for 'Barn Owl', 'Night Thoughts: Baby & Demon', 'Mother Who Gave Me Life' and 'Andante' from *Selected Poems* (1990), and for 'A Welcome: Flowers and Fowls' and 'The Twins' from *Bone Scan* (1988). DOROTHY HEWETT: The author for 'In Moncur Street' and 'Grave Fairytale' from *Rapunzel in Suburbia* (Prism Books, 1975), and 'Anniversary' from *Greenhouse* (Big Smoke Books, 1979). PHILIP HODGINS: Collins/Angus & Robertson Publishers for 'Making Hay' and 'Ich Bin Allein' from *Blood and Bone* (1986); the author for 'The Pier'. A. D. HOPE: Collins/Angus & Robertson Publishers for 'Advice to Young Ladies' from *Collected Poems* (1969), 'Country Places' and 'In Memoriam: Gertrud Kolmar, 1943' from *A Late Picking* (1975), and 'Inscription for a War' from *Antechinus* (1981). EVAN JONES: The author for 'The Point' from *Recognitions* (Australian National University Press, 1978); University of Queensland Press for 'Drinking with Friends' and 'Poem just after midnight: summer: at home' from *Left at the Post* (1984). NANCY KEESING: The author for 'Olympus' and 'Old Hardware Store, Melbourne' from *Hails and Farewells* (Edwards and Shaw, 1977). ANTIGONE KEFALA: Hale & Iremonger Pty Limited for 'Barbecue' from *European Notebook* (1988); the author for 'The Place' from *Thirsty Weather* (Outback Press, 1978). PETER KOCAN: The author for two sections from 'The Private Poems of Governor Caulfield' ('O'Shaughnessy' and 'I recognize it now as plain report'). GEOFFREY LEHMANN: Collins/Angus & Robertson Publishers for poem 20 from 'Ross' Poems', from *Ross' Poems* (1978); the author for 'Parenthood' from *Children's Games* (Collins/Angus & Robertson Publishers, 1990). TONY LINTERMANS: Scribe Publications for 'The Escape from Youth' and 'Heat' from *The Shed Manifesto* (1989). KATE LLEWELLYN: The author for 'Theatre' and 'Yellow Stockings' from *Trader Kate and the Elephants* (Friendly Street Poets, 1982); the author and Redress Press for 'Breasts' and 'Helen (1)' from *Luxury* (1985). MYRON LYSENKO: Management and Software Consultants Pty Ltd and the author for 'Living in Coburg' from *Coughing with Confidence* (1988). JENNIFER MAIDEN: The author for 'The Mother-in-law of the Marquis de Sade' from *Birthstones* (Angus & Robertson, 1978); Black Lightning Press and the author for 'Falling to Prettiness', 'The Green Side' and 'Space Invaders' from *The Trust* (1988). DAVID MALOUF: University of Queensland Press for 'Confessions of an Only Child', 'Between Towns' and 'An Ordinary Evening at Hamilton' from *Neighbours in a Thicket* (1974). CHRIS MANSELL: The author for 'Definition Poem: Pissed as a Parrot' from *Head, Heart, Stone* (Fling Poetry, 1982) and 'Overtime' from *Redshift/Blueshift* (Five Islands Press, 1988). PHILIP MARTIN: Longman Cheshire Pty Limited for 'Preserved' and 'A Certain Love' from *New and Selected Poems* (1988). JAMES McAULEY: Collins/Angus & Robertson Publishers and Norma McAuley for 'Pietà', 'Because' and 'Childhood Morning—Homebush' from *Collected Poems 1936-70* (1971), and 'Nocturne' from *Music Late at Night* (1976). ROGER McDONALD: University of Queensland Press for 'Two Summers in Moravia' and '1915' from *Airship* (1975). RHYLL McMASTER: The author for 'Birds' from *The Brineshrimp* (University of Queensland Press, 1972) and 'A Dream of Washed Hair' from *Washing the Money* (Angus & Robertson, 1986). PHILIP MEAD: University of Queensland Press for 'The Man and the Tree' from *This River is in the South* (1984); the author for 'Words which may be confounded, or Dewdrops from the Manse'. LES A. MURRAY: Collins/Angus & Robertson Publishers for 'The Breach', 'The Buladelah-Taree Holiday Song Cycle' and 'The Future' from *The Vernacular Republic* (1988); the author and Collins/Angus & Robertson Publishers for 'The Tin Wash Dish' from *Dog Fox Field* (1990). MARK O'CONNOR: Curtis Brown (Aust.) Pty Ltd for 'Turtles Hatching' from *Selected Poems* (Hale & Iremonger, 1986), 'Minnamurra Forest' from *The Great Forest* (Hale & Iremonger, 1989), and 'The Jigsaw Woman'. OODGEROO NOONUCCAL: Jacaranda Wiley for 'We are Going', 'No More Boomerang' and 'Gifts' from *My People* (1970). JAN OWEN: The author for 'Mirror Image' and 'Young Woman Gathering Lemons' from *Boy with a Telescope* (Angus & Robertson, 1986). Collins/Angus & Robertson Publishers for 'Metro' from *Fingerprints on Light* (1990). GEOFF PAGE: Collins/Angus & Robertson Publishers for 'Grit' from *Cassandra Paddocks* (1980) and 'Clarence Lyric' from *Footwork* (1988). PETER PORTER: Oxford University Press for 'The Sadness of the Creatures', 'On First Looking into Chapman's Hesiod', 'The Lying Art' and 'The Easiest Room in Hell' from *Collected Poems* (1983). JENNIFER RANKIN: Martin Secker & Warburg for 'Cicada Singing' and 'Sea-bundle' from *Earth Hold* (1978). ELIZABETH RIDDELL: Collins/Angus & Robertson Publishers for 'Security' and 'Possibilities in an Airplane' from *From the Midnight Courtyard* (1989). ISOBEL ROBIN: The author for 'Freud's Back-yard' and 'Frogs' Eggs'. JUDITH RODRIGUEZ: University of Queensland Press for 'About this woman:', 'Water a Thousand Feet Deep,' 'Eskimo Occasion', 'A Concerned Aerial View' and 'In-flight Note' from *New and Selected Poems* (1988). GIG RYAN: The author for 'If I Had a Gun' from *The Division of Anger* (Transit Poetry, 1980) and 'Two Winters'; Hale and Iremonger Pty Limited for 'So What' from *Manners of an Astronaut* (1984). PHILIP SALOM: Fremantle Arts Centre Press for 'Bicentennial—Living Other Lives' and 'Bar Sonnet 1' from *Sky Poems* (1987); University of Queensland Press for 'Properties of the Poet' and 'The Chamber and Chamberlain' from *Barbecue of the Primitives* (1989). JOHN A. SCOTT: The author for 'Pride of Erin' from *The Quarrel with Ourselves & Confession* (Rigmarole Books, 1984); University of Queensland Press for 'Man in Petersham' and '"Changing Room"' from *Singles* (1989). MARGARET SCOTT: Collins/Angus & Robertson Publishers for 'Grandchild' and 'Elegies' (I, II, III, V) from *The Black Swans* (1988). THOMAS SHAPCOTT: University of Queensland Press for 'June Fugue', 'Near the School for Handicapped Children', 'Town Edge' and 'A Record of Flamenco Singing' from *Selected Poems* (1989). ALEX SKOVRON: The author for 'Beyond Nietzsche' and 'Schooldream'. VIVIAN SMITH: Collins/Angus & Robertson Publishers for 'For My Daughter' and 'The Man Fern near the Bus Stop' from *Tide Country* (1982); the author for 'Night Life'. EDITH SPEERS: Twelvetrees Publishing Co. for 'Australorp' from *By Way of a Vessel* (1986); the author for Sonnet 9 from 'Love Sonnets'. JENNIFER STRAUSS: The author for 'Loving Parents' and 'Songs Our Mothers Teach Us' from *Children and Other Stangers* (Thomas Nelson Australia, 1975); Pariah Press and the author for 'Bluebeard Re-Scripted Version III: Sister Anne, Her Story', 'Tending the Graves' and 'The Snapshot Album of the Innocent Tourist' from *Labour Ward* (1988). ANDREW TAYLOR: University of Queensland Press for 'A Nocturne in the Corner Phonebox' and 'An Unbelievably Tidy Profusion' from *Selected Poems* (1988). JOHN TRANTER: Hale & Iremonger Pty Limited for poem 64 from 'Crying in Early Infancy' and 'A Jackeroo in Kensington' from *Selected Poems* (1982); University of Queensland Press for 'Lufthansa', 'Poolside', 'Crosstalk' and 'South Coast after Rain, 1960' from *Under Berlin* (1988). DIMITRIS TSALOUMAS: University of Queensland Press for 'Prodigal', 'The Return', 'Message' and 'Postponement' from *The Book of Epigrams* (1985), and for 'Epilogue' from *Falcon Drinking* (1988). ROBERT WALKER: Mrs Linda Walker for 'Solitary Confinement' and 'Life Is Life' from *Up, Not Down, Mate!* (1981). CHRIS WALLACE-CRABBE: Oxford University Press for 'Amphibious' and 'That Radical Politics is Impossible' from *The Amorous Cannibal* (1985), and for 'Stuff Your Classical Heritage', 'Hinge' and poem II from 'Sonnets to the Left' from *I'm Deadly Serious* (1988). ANIA WALWICZ: Collins/Angus & Robertson Publishers for 'Poland', 'Little Red Riding Hood' and 'fairytale' from *Boat* (1989). ALAN WEARNE: Penguin Books Australia Ltd for the extract (from 'You Can't Dine Out Forever') from *The Nightmarkets* (1986). FRANCIS WEBB: Collins/Angus & Robertson Publishers and A.L. Meere, C.M. Snell, Estate Late M.A. Web-Wagg for 'Harry', 'A Man', 'Nessun Dorma' and 'Lament for St Maria Goretti' from *Selected Poems* (1991). JUDITH WRIGHT: Collins/Angus & Robertson Publishers for 'A Document', 'Eve to Her Daughters' and 'Portrait' from *Collected Poems 1942-70* (1971), 'Tableau' from *Alive* (1973), and 'Smalltown Dance', 'Skins' and 'Oppositions' from *Phantom Dwelling* (1985). FAY ZWICKY: University of Queensland Press for 'Mrs Noah Speaks' from *Kaddish and Other Poems* (1982); the author and Australian Literary Management for 'Tiananmen Square' from *Ask Me* (University of Queensland Press, 1990).

Index of Poems

Index of Poets